Roadmap to the Ohio Graduation Test
Mathematics

educators.princetonreview.com

Roadmap
to the Ohio Graduation Test
Mathematics

by
Diane Perullo

Random House, Inc.
New York

www.randomhouse.com/princetonreview

 This workbook was written by The Princeton Review, one of the nation's leaders in test preparation. The Princeton Review helps millions of students every year prepare for standardized assessments of all kinds. The Princeton Review offers the best way to help students excel on standardized tests.

The Princeton Review is not affiliated with Princeton University or Educational Testing Service.

The Princeton Review, Inc.
160 Varick Street, 11th Floor
New York, NY 10013
E-mail: textbook@review.com

Copyright © 2005 by The Princeton Review, Inc.

All rights reserved under International and Pan-American Copyright Convention.

Published in the United States by Random House, Inc., New York.
ISBN 0-375-76518-2

Series Editor: Russell Kahn
Content Editor: Russell Kahn
Development Editor: Sherine Gilmour
Production Editor: Diahl Ballard
Production Coordinator: Robert Kurilla
Art Director: Neil McMahon
Design Director: Tina McMaster

Manufactured in the United States of America

9 8 7 6 5 4 3 2 1

First Edition

DEDICATION

Many thanks to my editor, Russell Kahn, whose continued support and kindness are deeply appreciated.

This book is dedicated with love to my daughter-in-law Nicole, with whose gentle guidance special needs children blossom and flourish.

CONTENTS

Introduction 1

Test-Taking Tips and Techniques 9
    Answering Multiple-Choice Questions 11
    Answering Short-Answer and Extended-Response Questions 15
    Test-Taking Tips 19

Lessons 21
    Lesson 1: Numbers and Operations 23
    Lesson 2: Scientific Notation and Exponents 29
    Lesson 3: Ratio, Proportion, and Percent 35
    Lesson 4: Perimeter, Circumference, Area, and Volume 41
    Lesson 5: Right Triangle Trigonometry 49
    Lesson 6: Similarity and Congruence 55
    Lesson 7: Geometric Figures and Coordinate Grids 61
    Lesson 8: Angles and Lines 69
    Lesson 9: Transformations 75
    Lesson 10: Patterns and Sequences 83
    Lesson 11: Functions and Equations 89
    Lesson 12: Inequalities 97
    Lesson 13: Quadratic Equations 103
    Lesson 14: Systems of Equations 109
    Lesson 15: Representing Data 115
    Lesson 16: Data Samples and Mean, Median, and Mode 121
    Lesson 17: Probability, Permutations, and Combinations 127

Answer Key for Lessons 133

Practice Tests 141
    Answer Document for Practice Test 1 149
    Practice Test 1 155
    Answer Document for Practice Test 2 189
    Practice Test 2 195

Answers and Explanations for Practice Tests 229
    Answers and Explanations for Practice Test 1 231
    Answers and Explanations for Practice Test 2 247

INTRODUCTION

ABOUT THIS BOOK

Roadmap to the Ohio Graduation Test: Mathematics is designed to help you prepare for the Ohio Graduation Test (OGT) for mathematics in the following two ways:

- by reinforcing your understanding of concepts and skills in mathematics as they are outlined by the Ohio K–12 Mathematics Benchmarks and Indicators
- by providing you with plenty of practice questions that are similar to the questions you will have to answer on the actual test

Before you make your way through this book, take a look at the table of contents and skim through the pages to get an idea of what to expect. (Don't look at the answers to the questions, though!) You might discover that you feel more comfortable with some mathematical skills than you do with others. We recommend that you complete *all* the lessons, but if you don't have enough time, focus your attention on the lessons that relate to those mathematical skills that are new to you or that have been difficult for you in the past.

A description of each of the components of the book follows.

LESSONS

Each of the seventeen lessons in this book addresses a set of concepts and skills as outlined by the Ohio K–12 Mathematics Benchmarks and Indicators. The Math OGT is designed to test your understanding of the concepts and skills identified in these Benchmarks and Indicators.

The Benchmarks and Indicators that each lesson reviews are identified at the beginning of the lesson. You can find a complete list of the Benchmarks and Indicators by going online to www.ode.state.oh.us/academic_content_standards/ and then clicking on Mathematics, then Academic Content Standards. Each lesson includes

- *About This Benchmark*: a description of how the concepts and skills may be practically tested on the OGT
- *Vocabulary Review*: a review of vocabulary terms essential to the skills addressed in the lesson
- *Sample*: a sample question like one you may see on the actual OGT
- *How to Answer*: a step-by-step demonstration of how to answer the sample question, using test-taking strategies
- *Tips*: pointers about the OGT for math, concepts and skills in mathematics, and test-taking in general
- *Now You Try It!*: practice questions for you to answer on your own, in the style and format of the actual OGT

ANSWER KEYS FOR THE LESSONS

You can check your answers to all questions in the *Now You Try It!* sections of the lessons in the answer keys that begin on page 135. The answer key provides the correct answer to each question. *Do not read the answers before you try the questions yourself.* It is better to try your best on your own and then compare your work with the answers afterward.

THE PRACTICE TESTS

This book includes two full-length practice tests, modeled in structure and content to an actual Math OGT. These practice tests give you a chance to take your refreshed understanding of mathematics for a test drive. The instructions for taking the practice tests are on page 143. Read the instructions completely before you take the tests. Be sure that you treat the practice tests like the actual OGT; don't take a break in the middle of the test, and avoid distractions like television, music, or the phone. And be sure to use the separate answer document to log your answers on the practice tests.

ANSWERS AND EXPLANATIONS FOR THE PRACTICE TESTS

You can check your answers to all practice test questions in the answers and explanations that begin on page 233 and page 249. In addition to correct answers, this section provides explanations for why the answers are correct. Be sure to read every explanation—even for the questions that you answered correctly. Even if you chose the right answer to a question, you may learn something important by reading the explanation to the question in this section.

ABOUT THE MATH OHIO GRADUATION TEST

Soon, all public high school students in the state of Ohio must take each of the OGT tests to receive a high school diploma. There are five OGT tests: mathematics, reading, science, social studies, and writing. In order to earn a high school diploma, you need to pass all of the OGT tests.

Even if you have already passed all the courses that you need for your diploma, you must take and pass all of the OGT tests.

WHAT IS THE PURPOSE OF THE MATH OGT?

The Math OGT is used to show that Ohio public high school students have mastered the concepts and skills that the state has determined are essential for graduation. Passing the Math OGT is necessary to receive an Ohio high school diploma.

FREQUENTLY ASKED QUESTIONS

CAN I RETAKE THE MATH OGT IF I DO NOT PASS?
Yes. You can retake the Math OGT until you pass it in order to earn your diploma.

WHEN IS THE MATH OGT ADMINISTERED?
The Math OGT is first administered in the spring of your sophomore year. But you may take a retest several times throughout your junior and senior years, if necessary.

WHAT'S ON THE MATH OGT?
The Math OGT tests how well you understand the concepts and skills outlined in the Ohio K–12 Mathematics Benchmarks and Indicators. The concepts and skills you have been learning in your mathematics classes are also based on the Ohio K–12 Mathematics Benchmarks and Indicators.

HOW IS THE MATH OGT STRUCTURED?
- The Math OGT includes 44 questions. Of those 44 questions, most are multiple-choice questions, few are short-response questions, and a few are extended-response questions. (See pages 15–19 for more information about short-answer and extended-response questions.)
- Each multiple-choice question offers four answer choices from which you select the correct answer. You record your answers to multiple-choice questions by filling in bubbles on an answer sheet. All multiple-choice questions have answer choices A, B, C, and D.

WHAT TOOLS CAN I USE ON THE OGT?
You will have several important tools for your use when you take the OGT for math. Be sure you have these tools when you work through this book, so you'll be familiar with those tools when it is time to take the actual OGT. You will have the following tools:
- A mathematics reference sheet: This reference sheet will provide important formulas. See page 7 to see what the mathematics reference sheet will look like. It helps to know these formulas by heart, but you *will* have access to them when you take the OGT. You may want to cut out the following formula sheet to use with the lessons.
- A scientific calculator: You will be provided with a scientific calculator when you take the OGT for math. You will only be allowed to use the calculator provided to you during the actual test.

Introduction

How Do I Approach the Test?

- **Pace yourself.** When you sit down to take the test, take a deep breath, relax, and focus. You will have up to two and a half hours to complete the Math OGT. There is no need to rush through questions. If you work too quickly, you are more likely to make careless mistakes. Instead, pace yourself by working carefully through each question. When there's a question that you can't answer, don't get stuck and get frustrated. Skip it and come back to answer it later. It's better to move on to other questions that you might find easier. Just be sure to keep track of your answers on the answer document!

- **Take your best guess.** When you reach the end of the test, there will probably be some questions that you had to skip. Make sure you go back and answer every question before handing in your test! Any question left blank will be marked wrong, so it's better to take your best guess and maybe get the question correct than to leave it blank and guarantee that you'll get it incorrect.

- **Check your work.** You don't get any extra points for finishing quickly, so it's better to double-check as many of your answers as you can. Make sure you didn't make any silly mistakes, like filling in the wrong answer bubble!

- **Be comfortable.** It's important to feel rested and comfortable on the testing day in order to do your best. Try to get plenty of sleep for several nights before the test. Make sure to eat well on the day you take the test. Be prepared: bring several pencils, a sharpener, a calculator, a ruler, a watch, and tissues (if you need them). Use the bathroom just before test time.

For More Information

Check with the Ohio Department of Education for the most recent information about when the Math OGT is given, how it is scored, and what's on it. Visit their Web site for updates: www.ode.state.oh.us/. You can find all of the Benchmarks and Indicators used in this book by opening the document entitled Benchmarks and Indicators by Grade Level at www.ode.state.oh.us/academic_content_standards/acsmath.asp. A section of this document is devoted to the Benchmarks and Indicators for grades 8 through 10.

Ohio Graduation Test Mathematics - Reference Sheet

Area Formulas

parallelogram $A = bh$

rectangle $A = lh$

trapezoid $A = \frac{1}{2}h(b_1 + b_2)$

trapezoid $A = \frac{1}{2}bh$

Circle Formulas

$C = 2\pi r$ $\quad \pi \approx 3.14$ or $\frac{22}{7}$

$A = 2\pi r^2$

Volume Formulas

cone $\quad V = \frac{1}{2}\pi r^2 h$

cylinder $\quad V = \pi r^2 h$

pyramid $\quad V = \frac{1}{3}Bh \quad B = $ area of base

rectangular prism $\quad V = lwh$

right prism $\quad V = Bh \quad B = $ area of base

sphere $\quad V = \frac{4}{3}\pi r^3$

Combinations

$_nC_r = C(n,r) = \frac{n!}{r(n-r)n!}$

Permutations

$_nP_r = P(n,r) = \frac{n!}{(n-r)!}$

Distance Formula

$d = \sqrt{(x_2 - x_1)^2 + (y_2 - y_1)^2}$

Quadratic Formula

$x = \frac{-b \pm \sqrt{b^2 - 4ac}}{2a}$

Trigonometry

$\sin A = \frac{opposite}{hypotenuse}$

$\cos A = \frac{adjacent}{hypotenuse}$

$\tan A = \frac{opposite}{adjacent}$

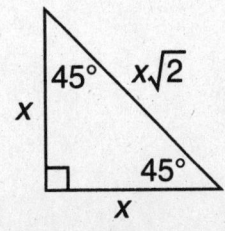

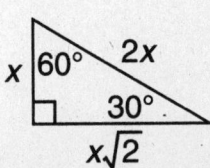

Mathematics Reference Sheet

Test-Taking Tips and Techniques

ANSWERING MULTIPLE-CHOICE QUESTIONS

Most of the questions on the Math Ohio Graduation Test (OGT) are multiple choice. Each multiple-choice question gives you four answer choices, labeled **A**, **B**, **C**, and **D**, and you have to pick the best one. Once you have made your choice, you fill in a bubble that corresponds with your choice. Consider following the following steps when answering multiple-choice questions.

Step 1 Read the question carefully and make sure you understand what it is asking.

By reading carefully, you should be able to determine exactly what the question is asking. It may help to underline numbers and other information in the question that you need to find the answer. In addition, it is a good idea to underline such words as *approximate*, *total*, *closest*, *best*, *least*, *most*, and other similar words. *If*, *then*, *and*, and *or* are important too! Those words tell you what kind of answer you are looking for or tell you what operation to use.

Step 2 Choose a problem-solving strategy.

Problem-solving strategies include the following possibilities:

- Write and solve an equation or equations.
- Draw a diagram.
- Create a chart or graph.
- Look for a pattern.
- List all possibilities.
- "Plug in" a value, or try out a special case.
- Work backward.
- Guess and check.
- Create and solve a simpler problem.

Some strategies may be more appropriate for particular types of questions than for others. You may also feel more comfortable using certain strategies than you do using others. The practice questions in this book offer you many opportunities to find out what works best for you!

Test-Taking Tips and Techniques

Step 3 Find your answer.

Work carefully as you solve the problem.

- Compare the information that you have written in your work to the information that is in the question to make sure that you didn't mistakenly write the information incorrectly.
- Write clearly so that you can read your work.
- Label, label, label! Label all numbers and units as you work through the problem so that when you check your work you can recall your thought process.

Step 4 Check your answer.

You can check your answer using many methods.

- Review your answer.
- Make sure that your answer is reasonable. For example, perhaps you chose 50° for the measure of the third angle in a triangle in which the other two angles each measure 80°. Because 50° would make the sum of the measures of the angles of the triangle add up to 210°, 50° is too high and is incorrect. (The measures of the angles in a triangle must add up to 180°!)
- Find an estimated answer by rounding the information in the question. For example, given the information that two angles add up to 180° and that one angle is 71°, you can round 71 to 70. Then you know that the correct answer must be close to 180° − 70°, or 110°.

Step 5 Read all the answer choices. If necessary, use Process of Elimination.

You may believe that you have identified the correct answer before reading through all of the answer choices. However, read through *all* the answer choices to be sure that you have identified the *best* answer choice. Sometimes you will find another answer choice that makes more sense. Draw a line through answer choices that you know are incorrect. That way you won't waste time reconsidering choices you already decided are wrong.

Even if you're not sure of the correct answer, you can still find the correct choice to a multiple-choice question. How? By using Process of Elimination (POE)! POE means getting rid of answer choices that you can tell are probably incorrect. Use the information in the question, calculations, estimates, or your knowledge of mathematics to eliminate incorrect answer choices.

If you can eliminate three answer choices, you will have only one choice left. Select this choice because there is a good chance that it is the correct answer. Even if you can only eliminate one or two of the answer choices, you're in good shape. Just take your best guess from the remaining answer choices. By eliminating even one answer choice, you have increased your chances of identifying the correct answer.

Step 6   Record your answer choice in the appropriate space on your answer document.

Circle the correct answer choice in your test booklet so that you will remember which choice you decided was correct. Carefully fill in the appropriate bubble on your answer document, making sure that you are filling in the space for the correct question number and the correct answer choice.

PRACTICING THE STEPS

Now practice using the steps on this sample multiple-choice question.

▶ The Transportation Authority surveyed the airline companies that flew out of Public Airport. They found that 0.3 of those surveyed used Airline A, 6 out of every 24 surveyed used Airline B, 40% of those surveyed used Airline C, and the remainder used Airline D. What fraction of the people surveyed used Airline D?

A. $\dfrac{1}{25}$

B. $\dfrac{1}{20}$

C. $\dfrac{1}{4}$

D. $\dfrac{1}{5}$

Test-Taking Tips and Techniques

Step 1 Read the question carefully and make sure you understand what it is asking.

You can see that the question is using different forms of real numbers for you to interpret. You may want to underline each of the real numbers, as well as the words *fraction* and *used Airline D*.

Step 2 Choose a problem-solving strategy.

You may decide to solve this problem by expressing each number in the same form, such as a percent. In the next step, you will see how this is done.

Step 3 Find your answer.

First, you need to take each number and find the equivalent percent.

Take them in the order they are given in the question. The number of people using Airline A is $0.3 = \frac{30}{100} = 30\%$. The number of people using Airline B is 6 out of $24 = \frac{6}{24} = \frac{1}{4} = 0.25 = 25\%$. The number of people using Airline C is already in the percent form, 40%.

The next part of the question is to find the number of people surveyed that used Airline D. Add the percents you've gotten so far: 30% + 25% + 40% = 95%. Now subtract from the entire number surveyed or 100%: 100 − 95 = 5%. 5% of the people surveyed use Airline D.

Step 4 Check your answer.

You should always check your calculations. In this case, the answer in Step 3 is correct.

Step 5 Read all the answer choices. If necessary, use Process of Elimination.

Answer choice **A** is $\frac{1}{25}$, which is the same as 0.04, or 4%. This is incorrect. Draw a line through it. Answer choice **B** is $\frac{1}{20}$, which is the same as 0.05, or 5%. This looks like the right answer choice. Look at the others, just to be sure. Answer choice **C** is $\frac{1}{4}$, which is the same as 0.25, or 25%. That's not right. Draw a line through it. Answer choice **D** is $\frac{1}{5}$, which is the same as 0.2, or 20%. That's incorrect. Draw a line through it.

Step 6 Record your answer choice in the appropriate space on your answer document.

On the day of the test, you would circle **B** on your test. Then, you would carefully fill in the appropriate bubble, making sure that you are filling in the space for the correct question number and the correct answer choice.

ANSWERING SHORT-ANSWER AND EXTENDED-RESPONSE QUESTIONS

You will need to know how to answer short-answer and extended-response questions for the grade Math OGT. Both short-answer and extended-response questions require that you write your answer and show your calculations. Extended-response questions usually require more work and more calculations to solve than short-answer questions. You will calculate the answer on graphing paper for each short-answer and extended-response question and write your answer on graphing paper in a separate answer document. Consider following these steps when answering short-answer and extended-response questions.

Step 1 Read the question carefully and make sure you understand what it is asking.

By reading carefully, you should be able to determine exactly what the question is asking. It may help to underline numbers and other information in the question that you need to find the answer. In addition, it is a good idea to underline such words as *approximate, total, closest, best, least, most,* and other similar words. *If, then, and,* and *or* are important too! Those words tell you what kind of answer you are looking for or tell you what operation to use.

Step 2 Choose a problem-solving strategy.

Problem-solving strategies include the following possibilities:
- Write and solve an equation or equations.
- Draw a diagram.
- Create a chart or graph.
- Look for a pattern.
- List all possibilities.
- "Plug in" a value or try out a special case.
- Work backward.
- Guess and check.
- Create and solve a simpler problem.

Some strategies may be more appropriate for particular types of questions than for others. You may also feel more comfortable using certain strategies than you do using others. The practice questions in this book offer you many opportunities to find out what works best for you!

Step 3 Find your answer.

Work carefully as you solve the problem.

- Compare the information that you have written in your work to the information that is in the question to make sure that you didn't mistakenly write the information incorrectly.
- Write clearly so that you can read your work.
- Label, label, label! Label all numbers and units as you work through the problem so that when you check your work you can recall your thought process.

Step 4 Check your answer.

You can check your answer using many methods.

- Review your answer.
- Make sure that your answer is reasonable. For example, perhaps you chose 45° for the measure of the third angle in a triangle in which the other two angles each measure 75°. Because 45° would make the sum of the measures of the angles of the triangle add up to 195°, 45° is too high and therefore must be incorrect. (The measures of the angles in a triangle must add up to 180°!)
- Round the information in the question to find an estimate using the rounded information. For example, given the information that two angles add up to 180° and that one angle is 71°, you can round 71 to 70. Then you know that the correct answer must be close to 180° – 70°, or 110°.

Step 5 Write your answer and show your calculations on the answer document.

Write down the correct answer in your test booklet so that you will remember the answer at which you arrived. Carefully write your calculations and the correct in the appropriate space on your answer document. The answer document will provide graphing paper for all short-answer and extended-repsonse questions.

Make sure that you have clearly and completely answered the question.

PRACTICING THE STEPS

Now practice using the steps on this short-answer question.

▶ A vending machine company has determined that the profits from one of its machines can be found by using the equation $P = 12c + 20s$, where P is the profit, in cents, c is the number of bags of chips sold, and s is the number of cans of soda sold.

A vending machine in the ABC Manufacturing Company sold 48 bags of chips and 63 cans of soda. A vending machine in XYZ Sand Company sold 83 bags of chips and 41 cans of soda.

Determine which vending machine had the greater profit and how much more profit that machine earned. Show your work or provide and explanation for your answer.

Step 1 Read the question carefully and make sure that you understand what it is asking.

By reading carefully, you should be able to determine that this question wants you to solve two equations and compare the answers.

Step 2 Choose a problem-solving strategy.

You may decide to solve this problem by plugging the given values into the equation, one at a time.

Step 3 Find your answer.

You've been given the equation $P = 12c + 20s$, as well as information from two different vending machines. The ABC Manufacturing Company vending machine sold 48 bags of chips and 63 cans of soda. Plug those values into the equation.

$$P = 12(48) + 20(63)$$
$$P = 576 + 1,260$$
$$P = 1,836$$

The first vending machine had a profit of 1,836 cents, or $18.36.

The XYZ Sand Company vending machine sold 83 bags of chips and 41 cans of soda.

$$P = 12(83) + 20(41)$$
$$P = 996 + 820$$
$$P = 1,816$$

The second vending machine had a profit of 1,816 cents, or $18.16.

The last part of the question wants you to find how much more profit there was so you would subtract the lesser profit from the greater profit. $18.36 − $18.16 = $0.20.

The ABC Manufacturing Company vending machine had the greater profit by $0.20.

Step 4 Check your answer.

Make sure that you've plugged the right numbers into each of the equations. Then recheck your calculations to make sure that they are correct. Be sure to note that the problem states the answer in cents, so the final answer is either $0.20, or 20 cents.

Step 5   Write your answer and show your calculations on the answer document.

To receive the full credit for this question, you have to show both equations. You also have to show how you found the difference in the two profits. A simple sentence like "The ABC Manufacturing Company vending machine had the greater profit by $0.20" would complete this answer for you and give you full credit.

Remember that all open-ended questions will give you graphing paper for your repsonse. It does **not** mean you have to graph anything!

TEST-TAKING TIPS

Here are some tips that may help you on the *Math Ohio Graduation Test*.

- Work carefully and review your work to avoid making accidental errors.
- Label your work. Always write the units in your calculations.
- For multiple-choice questions, always read all of the answer choices before choosing an answer. Sometimes the first or second answer choice seems correct until you find an even better answer choice below it.
- Always refer to the original problem while you pick an answer choice. Double-checking your answer choice this way helps you avoid accidentally picking the wrong choice.
- If a question is difficult, don't look for the best answer choice right away. Instead, eliminate all of the answer choices that contain one or more errors, and then choose the best answer from the remaining choices.
- Mark an answer to question, even if you aren't sure of the correct answer. The *Ohio Graduation Test* does not reduce your score for wrong answers, so it's better to guess than to leave a question blank.
- Write in the test booklet if it helps you. Writing given information on the diagrams can make it easier to solve.
- Keep in mind that diagrams in the *Ohio Graduation Test* are not always drawn to scale.
- Bring several sharpened pencils and erasers. You will be supplied with a calculator.

Here is some general advice to make sure that you are comfortable during any test you'll take.

- Sleep well every night for a full week before the test.
- Eat a good breakfast (and lunch).
- Dress in layers so you can adapt to the testing room conditions.
- Consider the test important, but not the most important event of the year. Keep it in perspective.

LESSON 1
NUMBERS AND OPERATIONS

> NUMBER, NUMBER SENSE, AND OPERATIONS B, C, D, E, AND F

About This Benchmark

You will have to understand the real number system and be able to compare and order equivalent forms of real numbers. You will practice applying the properties of operations.

VOCABULARY REVIEW

The **real number system** is the set of all rational numbers and irrational numbers.

A **rational number** is a number that can be expressed as a ratio of two integers where the denominator is not 0. For example, $\frac{3}{5}$ is a rational number. 0.5 is also a rational number because it is equivalent to $\frac{1}{2}$, which is a ratio of two numbers where the denominator is not 0.

An **irrational number** is a number that cannot be expressed as the ratio of two numbers. When an irrational number is expressed as a decimal, it is nonrepeating and nonterminating. For example, pi is an irrational number because pi is a nonrepeating, unending number starting with 3.14159265....

An **integer** is a positive or negative whole number. Zero is also an integer.

An **operation** is a mathematical process. Addition, subtraction, multiplication, and division are all operations.

The diagram below shows some examples of rational and irrational numbers.

Rational Numbers	Irrational Numbers
$\frac{3}{5}$ (Integers: −23, 6, 0) 0.5 0.$\overline{7}$ −1.6	π 1.6066951... $\sqrt{2}$ $-\frac{\pi}{2}$ $\sqrt{7}$

Lesson 1: Numbers and Operations

Multiple-Choice Sample

▶ Which number below is rational?

A. $\sqrt{57}$

B. $0.2272727272\overline{727}$

C. $-0.232232223\ldots$

D. 2π

How to Answer

Step 1 Read the question carefully and make sure you know what it's asking. You need to find the one term from the answer choices that is rational. You may have underlined the word rational.

Step 2 Choose a problem-solving strategy.

Recall the definition for the terms "rational number" and "irrational number." (Check the definitions on the previous page, if necessary.) For some of the answer choices, you should convert the values to tell if they are rational or irrational.

Step 3 Find your answer.

Go through each of the answers choices, one by one, to find the one which provides a rational number.

A. $\sqrt{57}$ is equal to $7.5498344352707\ldots$. This square root doesn't repeat or end so it's irrational. You can't represent this value as a fraction with two integers.

B. $0.2272727272\overline{727}$ is a repeating decimal. If it repeats, that means it is rational. You don't even have to convert it, although it is equal to $\frac{5}{22}$. This looks like the correct answer choice, but check the others to be sure.

C. $-0.232232223\ldots$ is a decimal that does not repeat or end. That fits the definition of an irrational number.

D. 2π uses the symbol π, which is an irrational number. Remember that pi cannot be represented as a fraction with two integers, and it never ends or repeats as a decimal. This value must be irrational.

Step 4 Check your answer.

Make sure that your answer fits the rules of a rational number. If you converted any of the numbers, do a quick review with your calculator.

Step 5 Read all the answer choices. If necessary, use Process of Elimination.

If you were not sure which value was rational, cross off the choices that include numbers that are definitely irrational. For example, π is always irrational, so you can eliminate answer choice **D** right away.

Step 6 Record your answer choice in the appropriate space on your answer document.

If this question were on your OGT, you should circle answer choice **B** in your test booklet and then correctly fill in the appropriate bubble on your answer document.

Short-Answer Sample

▶ Frederick lives in a neighborhood that has lawns of the exact same size. He is trying to determine how to charge his neighbors to mow their lawns.

Scenario 1: Frederick charges $10 per lawn and pays for all of the gas himself.

Scenario 2: Frederick charges $8 per lawn and adds a 20% fee per job for the gas costs.

Scenario 3: Frederick charges $9, plus $\frac{1}{10}$ of that charge per job for the gas costs.

Determine which of these scenarios will earn Frederick the most money. Show your work.

How to Answer

Step 1 Read the question carefully and make sure you understand what it is asking.

This question is asking you to determine which scenario is most profitable for Frederick. You might want to underline the important numbers in the problem, including the amount of charge (and additional fee, if there is one) for each scenario.

Lesson 1: Numbers and Operations

Step 2 Choose a problem-solving strategy.

You may choose to work on each scenario separately, finding the total amount that Frederick could earn for each one. If you write out each scenario as its own equation, you can solve for each one. You can solve for each lawn or for the total number of lawns because Frederick mows the same number of lawns in each scenario.

Step 3 Find your answer.

Take Scenario 1 first. Frederick's neighbors pay him $10 each. You don't know how much Frederick pays for gas, but that is not relevant to the question. Frederick earns $10 per lawn for Scenario 1.

For Scenario 2, Frederick collects $8 per lawn, plus a 20% fee for gas. 20% is equal to 0.20, so 0.20 × $8 = $1.60. Therefore, Frederick earns $8 + $1.60 per lawn. That is $9.60 per lawn for Scenario 2.

For Scenario 3, Frederick collects $9 for each lawn, plus $\frac{1}{10}$ for gas. Multiply $\frac{1}{10}$ by $9 to get $0.90. (You can convert $\frac{1}{10}$ to 0.10.) Then combine to get $9 + $0.90 to get $9.90. Frederick will collect $9.90 per lawn for Scenario 3.

Step 4 Check your answer.

You can calculate each of the scenarios again to make sure you haven't made an error. Is 20% of $8 equal to $1.60? Is $\frac{1}{10}$ of $9 equal to $0.90? Do not move on until you are satisfied with your answer.

Step 5 Write your answer and show your calculations on the answer document.

Carefully write your calculations and label them. Make sure that you state that Scenario 1 makes the greatest profit for Frederick. In the actual OGT, you would not get full credit for writing the correct answer (Scenario 1) unless you showed all your work! You could also earn credit for correct work, even if you did not arrive at the correct answer.

Tip!

It's easy to make a simple calculation error by forgetting to enter a digit in your calculator. You may also accidentally enter the decimal point in the wrong place. That's why it is important to use estimation and ballpark figures to check your calculations.

Now You Try It!

1. A plumber charges customer $38.00 per hour for her work, plus the cost of any parts she uses in making repairs. She charged the Henderson family $210.00 for a repair. The bill included a charge of $48.50 for parts.

   How long did it take the plumber to complete her repair? Show your work.

2. Which expression below is **not** equivalent to 11?

   A. $\sqrt{121}$

   B. $|-11|$

   C. $\dfrac{143}{13}$

   D. 11^0

3. The *Central City Gazette* reported the results of a snowstorm over a three-day period.

   Thursday: Snowstorm Devastates County: 12,000 homes lose electrical power.

   Friday: Some Power Restored: $\dfrac{1}{3}$ of the affected home have had their power restored.

   Saturday: More Snow: 25% of the homes that had restored power on Friday lost it again today.

   Determine how many homes were without power on Saturday. Show your work.

Lesson 1: Numbers and Operations

4. Which number is irrational?

   A. $\sqrt{484}$

   B. −201.3

   C. 0.35127932 . . .

   D. $\dfrac{3}{41}$

5. Bob works as a waiter. He gets taxed 30% on his wages but only 20% on his tips. He makes $200 from tips and $50 from wages before taxes.

   Determine how much Bob takes home after taxes. Show your work.

6. Which expression is **not** equivalent to 27?

   A. 27^1

   B. $\sqrt{739}$

   C. $\dfrac{108}{4}$

   D. 3^3

7. Which number is rational?
   A. 268.842842
   B. 487.129873 . . .
   C. $\sqrt{355}$
   D. π

LESSON 2
SCIENTIFIC NOTATION AND EXPONENTS

> NUMBER, NUMBER SENSE AND OPERATIONS A, H, AND I

About This Benchmark

You will use scientific notation to express large numbers and numbers smaller than one. Some questions on the OGT will ask you to find the square root of perfect squares and the approximate square root of non-perfect squares.

VOCABULARY REVIEW

Scientific notation is a way to write a number so that it is in the form $a \times 10^n$, where a is a number whose absolute value is between 1 and 10 and n is an integer. For example, the number 123,456,789 can be represented in scientific notation as 1.23456789×10^8.

A **square root** is one of the two equal factors of a number. For example, 4 is the square root of 16 because $4 \times 4 = 16$.

A **factor** is a number that is multiplied by another number or numbers to result in a product.

An **exponent** is the number that shows the number of times a base is used as a factor. In 5^3, the exponent is 3. That's because the base (5) is used as a factor three times ($5 \times 5 \times 5$).

Sample

▶ Which expression below represents 38,000 in scientific notation?

A. 3.8×10^3
B. 3.8×10^4
C. 3.8×10^5
D. 3.8×10^6

Lesson 2: Scientific Notation and Exponents

How to Answer

Step 1 Read the question carefully. You are to find the scientific notation that correctly expresses 38,000.

Step 2 First, remind yourself of the rules for reading numbers in scientific notation. When a number is expressed in scientific notation, it is written as a product of a factor and a power of 10.

Step 3 To convert 38,000 to scientific notation, you would make the factor a number between 1 and 10. In this case, it would be 3.8. Now count the number of places that you would move the decimal to the left to go from 38,000 to 3.8000. That's 4 places so the exponent is 4. 3.8×10^4.

Step 4 Check your answer. You could take the scientific notation and express it in standard form. Be sure to check the number of places that the decimal moves. You can even use your finger or your pencil to show how many places it moves.

$$3.8 \times 10^4 = 3.8000. = 38,000$$

Step 5 The answer in Step 3 and answer choice **B** are the same. You can check answer choices **A**, **C**, and **D** to see that they don't result in a value of 38,000.

Step 6 On the actual OGT, you will want to record your answer by carefully filling in the appropriate bubble in the answer document.

Tip!

Check whether the power of a factor is positive or negative. When working with scientific notation, if the power of 10 is positive, the standard form of the number will be larger than 10. If the power of 10 is negative, the standard form of the number will be smaller than 1.

Now You Try It!

1. Which expression represent 5.7×10^7 written in standard form?

    A. 57,000
    B. 570,000
    C. 5,700,000
    D. 57,000,000

2. Which is the square root of 676?

    A. 16
    B. 26
    C. 36
    D. 46

3. Which expression represents 0.0058 written in scientific notation?

    A. 5.8×10^{-3}
    B. 58×10^{-4}
    C. 580×10^{-5}
    D. $5,800 \times 10^{-6}$

4. The square root of 1,200 must be a number between which of the following?

    A. 24 and 25
    B. 28 and 29
    C. 30 and 31
    D. 34 and 35

Lesson 2: Scientific Notation and Exponents

5. Which expression represents 130,000 written in scientific notation?

   A. 1.3×10^3
   B. 1.3×10^4
   C. 1.3×10^5
   D. 1.3×10^6

6. Which number is closest to the square root of 899?

   A. 30
   B. 33
   C. 40
   D. 45

7. Which factor is correct if 37,200,000 is written in scientific notation?

   A. 372
   B. 37.2
   C. 3.72
   D. 0.372

8. Which expression represents 0.00000547 written in scientific notation?

   A. 547×10^{-8}
   B. 54.7×10^{-7}
   C. 5.47×10^{-6}
   D. 0.547×10^{-5}

9. Which is the correct estimate of the square root of 300?

   A. between 15 and 16
   B. between 17 and 18
   C. between 19 and 20
   D. between 20 and 21

10. Which is the correct estimate of the square root of a number between 150 and 160?

    A. between 10 and 11
    B. between 12 and 13
    C. between 13 and 14
    D. between 15 and 16

11. Which expression represents 6.4×10^{-5} in standard form?

    A. 0.0064
    B. 0.00064
    C. 0.000064
    D. 0.0000064

12. Which is the correct estimate of the square root of 2,499?

    A. 37
    B. 40
    C. 45
    D. 50

Lesson 2: Scientific Notation and Exponents

13. Which expression represents 0.000705 written in scientific notation?

   A. 7.05×10^{-4}
   B. 70.5×10^{-5}
   C. 705×10^{-6}
   D. 705.0×10^{-7}

14. Which is the correct estimate of the square root of a number between 601 and 729?

   A. between 16 and 19
   B. between 20 and 23
   C. between 24 and 27
   D. between 28 and 31

15. Which expression represents 8.33×10^{10} in standard form?

   A. 833,000,000
   B. 8,330,000,000
   C. 83,300,000,000
   D. 833,000,000,000

LESSON 3
RATIO, PROPORTION, AND PERCENT

> ACQUISITION OF VOCABULARY A

About This Benchmark
You will practice identifying proportional relationships in real-world situation. Some questions may ask you to use proportions and ratios to identify the correct answer. Other questions may ask you to use percentages.

VOCABULARY REVIEW

A **ratio** is a comparison of two or more quantities. A ratio can be expressed as $\frac{a}{b}$ or *a:b*.

A **percent** is a ratio that shows parts of a whole or parts of a group in terms of 100. A percentage uses the symbol %.

A **proportion** is an equation that shows that 2 ratios are equivalent. A proportion can be expressed by $\frac{a}{b} = \frac{c}{d}$.

Sample

▶ Last year, Ernie earned income from three sources. He earned $12,198 from photography jobs, $25,152 writing for a magazine, and $8,150 selling articles. After taxes, he kept $31,850 of his total income.

At what percent was his income taxed?

A. 30%

B. 33%

C. 45%

D. 70%

Lesson 3: Ratio, Proportion, and Percent

35

How to Answer

Step 1 Carefully read the question and decide what it is asking. You may have underlined the words *after taxes* and *percent*. This question is asking you to determine the percent at which Ernie's income was taxed.

Step 2 You might choose the strategy of creating and solving simpler problems.

Step 3 First, find Ernie's total income. Add together what Ernie made from photography, writing for a magazine, and selling articles: $12,198 + $25,152 + $8,150 = $45,500. Ernie's total income was $45,500. You know Ernie had $31,850 after taxes. You can use this data to determine the percentage of taxes taken from his total income. Find the difference between his total income and how much he had after taxes:

$45,500 − $31,850 = $13,650. Set up the fraction with the amount of taxes taken in the numerator and Ernie's total income in the denominator: $\frac{13,650}{45,500} = 0.30$. To convert a decimal to a percent, multiply the decimal by 100%: 0.30 × 100% = 30%. Ernie's total income was taxed at 30%.

Step 4 Check your answer. Find 30% of Ernie's total income by setting up ratios: $\frac{30}{100} = \frac{x}{45,500}$. Cross multiply: (30)($45,500) = (100)(x), or $1,365,000 = 100x. Now, divide both sides by 100 to determine how much 30% of Ernie's total income is: $\frac{\$1,365,000}{100} = \frac{100x}{100} = $13,650. Yes, you know that $13,650 is the amount taken from Ernie's income in taxes. Good work!

Step 5 Now, read all the answer choices.

Answer choice **A**, 30%, matches the percent from Step 3. This is probably the correct answer but read all the remaining answer choices to be sure. Answer choice **B**, 33%, does not match the percent from Step 3. This is not the correct answer. Draw a line through it. **C**, 45%, is too large to be the correct answer. If 45% of Ernie's $45,500 income was taken in taxes, then Ernie would have less than $31,850 left. Also, this does not match the percent from Step 3. Draw a line through it. And answer choice **D**, 70%, is the amount of money that Ernie had left over after taxes. But the question asked you to find the percent of taxes taken. This is not the correct answer. Draw a line through it.

Step 6 You determined that answer choice **A** is correct. So you would fill in the appropriate bubble on your answer document, making sure that you are filling in the space for the correct question number and the correct answer choice.

Tip!

A proportion can be written as two equal fractions. When you set up a proportion, make sure that the numerators and the denominators represent the same values in the fractions. Remember that you can solve a proportion by cross multiplying and then using your algebra skills to isolate the unknown.

Now You Try It!

1. The original price of a gold necklace was $400. The sale price is $300.

   What is the percent of decrease?

   A. 25%

   B. 33.3%

   C. 75%

   D. 133.3%

2. The table below shows the results of a survey in which 600 students were asked about the kind of television show they watch most. The school has 5,400 students.

   Most Watched Television Shows

Drama	50
Sitcom	200
Soap Opera	15
Reality Show	290
Game Show	30
Other	15

   How many students in the school population would be expected to watch mostly game shows?

   A. 135

   B. 270

   C. 450

   D. 1,800

Lesson 3: Ratio, Proportion, and Percent   37

3. A stock declined in value from $20 per share to $15 per share.

   What was the percent decrease?

   A. 25%
   B. 33.3%
   C. 75%
   D. 133.3%

4. The table below shows how 350 visitors to the county fair answered a survey about their favorite hamburger topping. There were 1,750 visitors to the county fair.

   Favorite Hamburger Topping

Onion	40
Lettuce	100
Tomato	35
Pickles	80
Ketchup	35
Mustard	60

   Out of all the visitors at the county fair, how many would be expected to choose pickles as their favorite topping?

   A. 320
   B. 400
   C. 480
   D. 1,400

5. The science club spends 65% of its annual club fund on camping trips. The members take 5 trips each year, spending equal amounts on each trip. Half of their expenses for their April trip consisted of transportation costs.

   What percentage of total annual club fund did the science club spend on transportation for their April trip?

   A. 6.5%

   B. 10%

   C. 13%

   D. 32.5%

6. The original price of a CD player was $90.00. The sale price is $49.50.

   What was the percent of decrease?

   A. 25%

   B. 45%

   C. 75%

   D. 133.3%

Lesson 3: Ratio, Proportion, and Percent

7. The table below shows the birthstones of 500 people who shopped at a jewelry store over the last 6 months. The total number of shoppers at the jewelry store during that time was 2,000.

Birthstones

Diamond	100
Sapphire	75
Ruby	95
Emerald	30
Opal	140
Amethyst	60

Out of all the shoppers, how many would be expected to have an emerald as their birthstone?

A. 60
B. 80
C. 100
D. 120

8. 560 school students were asked which place they would most like to visit from the 6 choices listed in the table below. The table also shows their choices.

Places You'd Like to Visit

Moon	120
Mars	80
Europe	110
Antarctica	10
Hawaii	40
The Great Wall of China	200

If 1,680 school students were surveyed, what would be the expected number of students who chose Mars based on the table?

A. 80
B. 160
C. 240
D. 320

LESSON 4
PERIMETER, CIRCUMFERENCE, AREA, AND VOLUME

> MEASUREMENT A, B, C, E, AND F

About This Benchmark

You will practice determining the perimeter, circumference, area, and volume of various figures and polygons. Some questions may ask you to find the area, surface area, or volume of 2- and 3-dimensional figures.

VOCABULARY REVIEW

A **2-dimensional** figure is a figure that has length and width.

A **3-dimensional** figure is a figure that has length, width, and height.

Perimeter is a measure of the distance around a 2-dimensional figure.

Circumference is a measure of the distance around a circle.

A **central angle** is the measure of the distance between two diameters that intersect at the center of a circle.

Area is the amount of space inside a 2-dimensional figure. Square units are used to express area.

Surface area is the sum of the areas of all surfaces of a 3-dimensional figure. Square units are used to express surface area.

Volume is the amount of space inside a 3-dimensional figure. Cubic units are used to express volume.

Lesson 4: Perimeter, Circumference, Area, and Volume

Multiple-Choice Sample

Margo has a cube-shaped storage box that has a volume of 64 cubic inches. She needs more storage, so she gets another box. The width and length of the new box are both double the size of the original storage box, and the height of the new box is half that of the height of the original box.

What is the volume of the new box?

- A. 32 inches^3
- B. 64 inches^3
- C. 96 inches^3
- D. 128 inches^3

How to Answer

Step 1 Read the question carefully. The question asks you to find the volume of a new box with different dimensions from the old box.

Step 2 You may choose to use the formula for the volume of a cube to identify the correct answer. (Refer to the reference sheet on page 7 for the formula of a cube.) You may also want to draw a diagram.

Step 3 First, use the volume of the cube to find the length of a side of the cube-shaped storage box. $V = s^3 = 64$ cubic inches. $\sqrt[3]{64} = 4$. Each side is 4 inches.

Now, make changes to the dimensions of the cube-shaped box to match those of the new box. The width is doubled, so $w = (2)(4 \text{ inches})$, or 8 inches. The length is doubled, so $l = (2)(4 \text{ inches})$, or 8 inches. The height is halved, so $h = \frac{1}{2}(4 \text{ inches})$, or 2 inches.

The new figure is a rectangular prism. Now, you can determine the volume of the new figure. The formula (as found on the reference sheet on page 7) is $V = lwh$. $V = 8 \text{ inches} \times 8 \text{ inches} \times 2 \text{ inches} = 128$ inches^3.

Step 4 Check your work. Make sure you have used the correct volume formulas, that the any diagram you may have drawn is correct, and that your calculations are correct. The calculations and formulas in Step 3 are correct.

Step 5 Now, read all the answer choices.

Answer choices **A**, **B**, and **C** do not match the answer from Step 3. Draw a line through them. **D**, 128 inches³, matches the answer from Step 3 and is correct.

Step 6 You determined that answer choice **D** is correct. So on the actual OGT, you would fill in the bubble for **D** in your answer document.

Short-Answer Sample

A new library floor is being installed in the local library. The library is 75 feet long and 125 feet wide. One corner is a tower with a radius of 15 feet, as shown below.

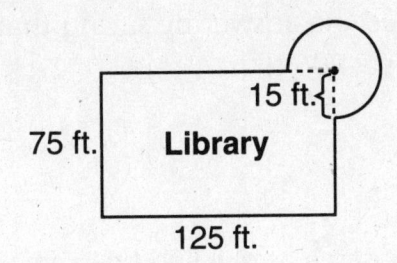

75 ft. | Library | 15 ft.
125 ft.

Find the approximate area in square feet of the new floor of the library.

How to Answer

Step 1 Read the question carefully. This question is asking you to find the *approximate* area of the rectangular library floor, as well as the corner tower. You may want to underline the word *approximate*.

Step 2 You may choose to use the formula for the area of a rectangle and the formula for the area of a circle. If you don't remember the formulas, refer to your reference sheet on page 7.

Step 3 The first step is to find the area of the rectangular floor. $A = lw =$ 75 ft × 125 ft = 9,375 ft². Next, find the area of the circular tower. $A = \pi r^2 =$ 3.14 × 15 ft² = 706.5 ft².

Now, it might seem easier to add the two areas together but notice that the circular part of the floor and a rectangular part of the floor overlap. The question is asking you to find the *approximate* area. By looking at the diagram, you can see that about one quarter of the circle overlaps the rectangle. So, you can subtract one quarter of the area of the circle. First, find one quarter of the area: 706.5 ft² ÷ 4 = 176.6 ft². Now subtract: 706.5 ft² − 176.6 ft² = 529.9 ft².

Lesson 4: Perimeter, Circumference, Area, and Volume

The last step is to add the two areas together: 9,375 ft² + 529.9 ft² = 9,904.9 ft², or approximately 9,905 ft².

Step 4 Check your work by checking your calculations and the use of the area formulas. You might want to check that your answer is reasonable by adding the areas of both the rectangle and circle (9,375 ft² + 706.5 ft² = 10,081.5 ft²) and see that your answer is slightly less, allowing for the overlapping area. The answer in **Step 3** is reasonable.

Step 5 Write your answer and show your calculations on the answer document. You would want to show the area formulas and your calculations, with everything clearly labeled. You would also want to make sure that you had clearly marked the answer by saying that the approximate area of the library floor is 9,905 ft².

Tip!

Multiplying by a fraction is the same as dividing by its inverse. So, if a problem requires you to multiply by $\frac{1}{3}$, you could also divide by 3. The result would be the same!

Remember that area is measured in square units or, units²; therefore, you must use 2 dimensions to determine area. Likewise, volume is measured in cubic units or, units³; so you must use 3 dimensions to determine values.

Now You Try It!

1. A circular pool has a radius of 10 feet.

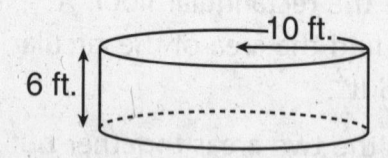

   About how much water is needed to fill the pool to a depth of 6 feet?

   A. 804 ft³
   B. 1,130 ft³
   C. 1,884 ft³
   D. 11,304 ft³

2. The diagram below shows the dimensions of a soccer field.

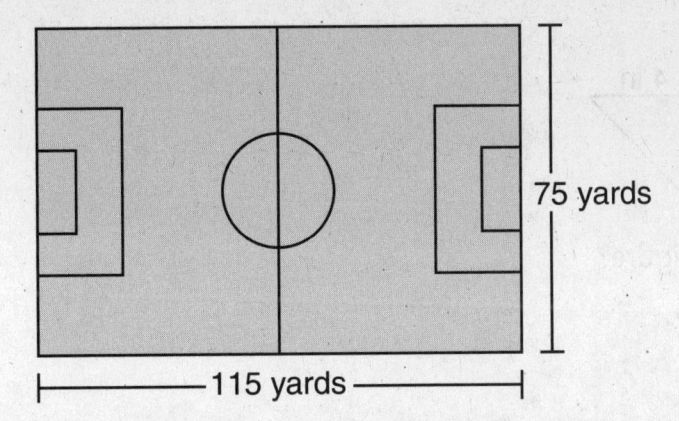

75 yards

115 yards

What is the perimeter of the soccer field?

A. 190 yards
B. 380 yards
C. 2,555 yards
D. 8,625 yards

3. Georgina used fencing to build a circular playpen for her puppy in her backyard. The radius of the playpen is 8 feet. What is the approximate circumference of the playpen?

A. 16 feet
B. 25 feet
C. 50 feet
D. 200 feet

Lesson 4: Perimeter, Circumference, Area, and Volume

4. The patio behind Micah's house is shaped like two triangles attached to a square, as in the diagram below.

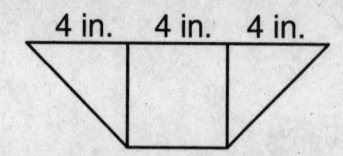

4 in.   4 in.   4 in.

What is the area of the figure?

A. 16 in²
B. 24 in²
C. 32 in²
D. 48 in²

5. Marilyn wants to cover the top and sides of a box with self-adhesive shelf paper. The box has the dimensions as in the diagram below.

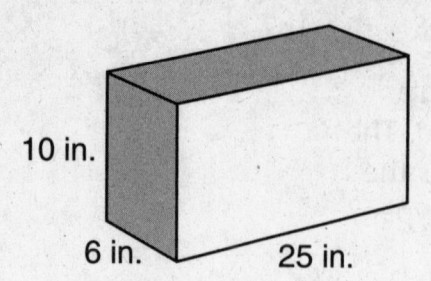

10 in.
6 in.   25 in.

Find the surface area in square feet of the top and the sides of the box. Show your work or explain how you found your answer.

6. Laura cut 25 paper rectangles, each with dimension 2 inches by 4 inches. She first lined up four of her rectangles, as shown in the diagram below.

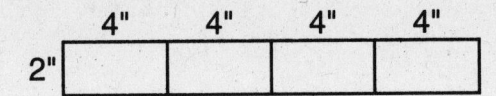

If Laura lined up all 25 of her paper rectangles, what would be the perimeter of the resulting figure, in inches?

A. 100 inches

B. 102 inches

C. 200 inches

D. 204 inches

7. A cube of ice has a side length of 18 inches as in the diagram below.

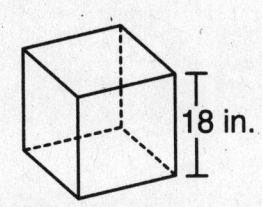

What is the volume of the cube of ice?

A. 18 in.^{3}

B. 324 in.^{3}

C. 972 in.^{3}

D. 5,832 in.^{3}

Lesson 4: Perimeter, Circumference, Area, and Volume

8. Henry ordered a pizza to share with three friends. The pie was divided into eight pieces.

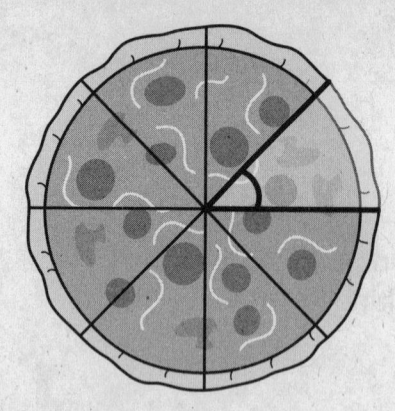

What is the approximate measure of the central angle shown?

A. 36°

B. 45°

C. 53°

D. 60°

9. A garden center is going to cement part of the floor of one of its buildings. The floor that will be cemented is square in the center and has 3 semicircles spaced around the square. The other semicircle will retain its current flooring.

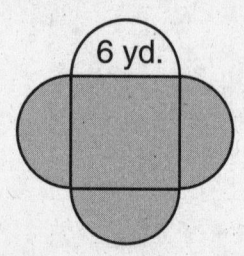

6 yd.

Find the approximate area, in square yards, of the floor that will be cemented. Show your work or explain how you found your answer.

LESSON 5
RIGHT TRIANGLE TRIGONOMETRY

> MEASUREMENT D

About This Benchmark

You will be using trigonometric ratios to solve problems involving right triangles.

VOCABULARY REVIEW

A **right triangle** has one angle that measure 90°.

A **right triangle ratio,** also known as a trigonometric ratio, is a ratio between two sides of a right triangle. Because there are 3 sides to every triangle, there are 6 right triangle ratios for every right triangle: sine, cosine, tangent, secant, cosecant, and cotangent.

The **hypotenuse** is the longest side of a right triangle.

The **legs** of a right triangle are the two sides of a right triangle other than the hypotenuse. Given a right triangle with certain known information, such as the lengths of two out of three sides or the measure of one of the angles (in addition to the right angle) and the length of one side, it is possible to determine all the other unknown pieces of information (the lengths of the remaining sides(s) and angles) using the following **trigonometric ratios**:

    The **sine** of an angle is the length of the leg opposite the angle divided by the length of the hypotenuse. Its abbreviation is sin.

    The **cosine** of an angle is the length of the leg adjacent to the angle divided by the length of the hypotenuse. Its abbreviation is cos.

    The **tangent** of an angle is the length of the leg opposite the angle divided by the length of the leg adjacent to the angle. Its abbreviation is tan.

    The **secant** of an angle is the hypotenuse divided by the length of the leg adjacent to the angle. Its abbreviation is sec.

    The **cosecant** of an angle is the length of the hypotenuse divided by the length of the leg opposite the angle. Its abbreviation is csc.

    The **cotangent** of an angle is the length of the leg adjacent to the angle divided by the length of the leg opposite the angle. Its abbreviation is cot.

The **Pythagorean theorem** states that in a right triangle the square of the length of the hypotenuse is equal to the sum of the squares of the measures of the other two sides: $c^2 = a^2 + b^2$.

Sample

The diagram below shows the dimensions of a right triangle.

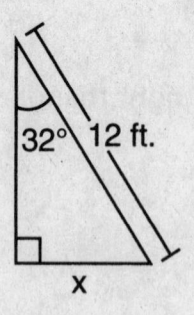

What is the approximate length of *x*?

   A. 5.3 feet

   B. 6.4 feet

   C. 7.1 feet

   D. 7.6 feet

How to Answer

Step 1   Carefully read the question. You may have underlined the word *approximate* and *x*.

Step 2   You may want to look at the definitions for the trigonometric ratios to see which one would help you solve this problem. You have the measure of an angle, the length of the hypotenuse, and you want to find the length of the leg opposite the angle. Sine would be a good ratio to use.

Step 3   Set up the sine ratio and plug in the values you've been given in the diagram. $\sin 32° = \frac{x}{12}$. Use your calculator to evaluate $\sin 32°$. $0.5299 = \frac{x}{12}$. Multiply by 12. $6.359 = x$. The approximate length of *x* is 6.4 feet.

Step 4 Check your answer. Make sure that you have set up the sine ratio correctly. Check your calculations. Another way to check your answer would be to round the 32° angle to 30° and then you would have a 30-60-90 triangle with the sides s-$s\sqrt{3}$ — $2s$. The side opposite the 90° angle is 12 feet ($2s$) so the side opposite the 30° angle would be s and approximately 6 feet. That makes your answer of 6.4 feet reasonable.

Step 5 Read all of the answer choices. Answer choice **B** matches the calculations found in Step 3 so it's probably the right answer. Check the others, just to be sure. Answer choice **A** is the evaluation of sin 32° without calculating the rest of the ratio. Draw a line through A. Answer choices **C** and **D** are too large and can't be right. Draw a line through them.

Step 6 You determined that answer choice **B** is correct. So you would fill in the appropriate bubble on your answer document, making sure that you are filling in the space for the correct question number and the correct answer choice.

Tip!

A simple way to remember the ratios for sine, cosine, and tangent is SOHCAHTOA. This mnemonic device helps you remember the first letter of each word in the ratios. SOH refers to sin-opposite-hypotenuse, CAH refers to cos-adjacent-hypotenuse, and TOA refers to tan-opposite-adjacent.

Lesson 5: Right Triangle Trigonometry

Now You Try It!

1. A sailboat is 110 feet away from the base of a building at the shore. The angle formed from the sailboat to the top of the building is 42 degrees.

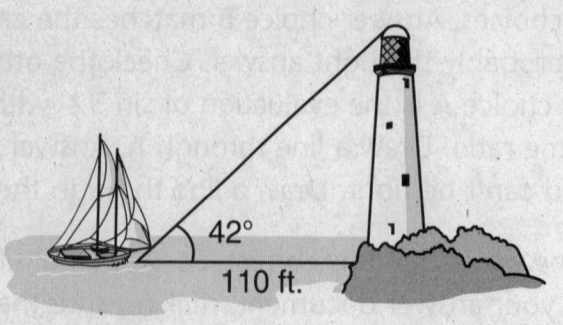

   42°
   110 ft.

   What is the approximate height, in feet, of the building?

   A. 42 feet
   B. 90 feet
   C. 99 feet
   D. 110 feet

2. The dimensions of a right triangle are shown in the diagram below.

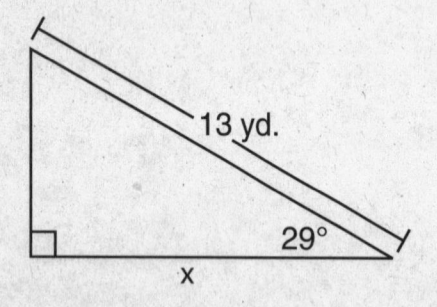

   13 yd.
   29°
   x

   What is the approximate length, in yards, of x?

   A. 11.4 yards
   B. 29.1 yards
   C. 46.5 yards
   D. 87.5 yards

Roadmap to the Ohio Graduation Test: Mathematics

3. The height of the pole in the triangle below is 60 feet. The angle of inclination is 24°.

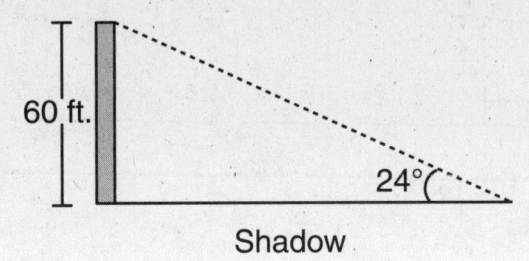

60 ft.

24°

Shadow

What is the approximate length, in feet, of the shadow?

A. 60 feet

B. 120 feet

C. 135 feet

D. 180 feet

4. A 20-foot ladder is leaning against a building. It forms a 68° angle with the ground, as in the diagram below.

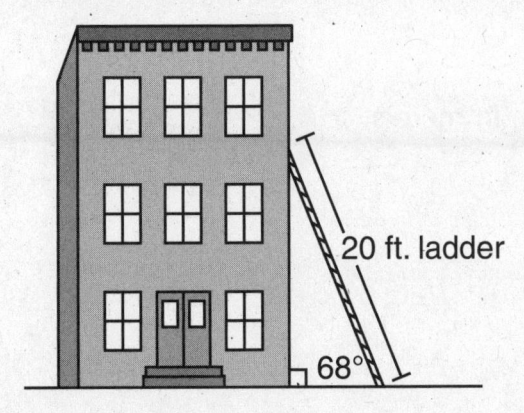

20 ft. ladder

68°

What is the approximate distance, in feet, of the base of the ladder from the building?

A. 3.7 feet

B. 7.5 feet

C. 13.5 feet

D. 20 feet

Lesson 5: Right Triangle Trigonometry

5. A ramp is built with a 6° incline. The length of the ramp is 15 feet.

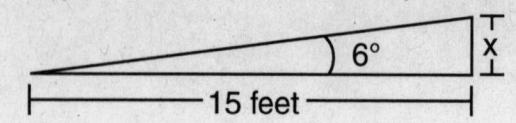

   What is the approximate height of the ramp, in feet, when it reaches the building?

   A. 0.5 feet
   B. 1.6 feet
   C. 2.0 feet
   D. 2.4 feet

6. The dimensions of a right triangle are shown in the diagram below.

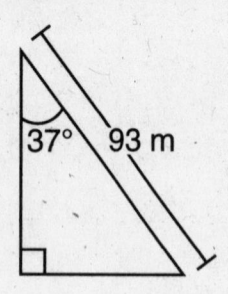

   What is the approximate length, in meters, of the base of the triangle?

   A. 27 meters
   B. 37 meters
   C. 42 meters
   D. 56 meters

LESSON 6
SIMILARITY AND CONGRUENCE

MEASUREMENT D AND GEOMETRY AND SPATIAL SENSE B

About This Benchmark

You will be using proportional reasoning as it applies to the properties of similar figures. You will practice using and understanding congruency. Some questions on the OGT may test your understanding of congruency to determine the area of figures.

VOCABULARY REVIEW

Similarity, in geometry, is the property of having the same shape, but not necessarily the same size.

Similar geometric figures may be different sizes, but their shapes are the same.

Congruency is the property two shapes have of being identical. Two congruent figures are identical in shape and size. Angles and line segments can share congruency as well. Congruent line segments are denoted with the same number of marks, as shown in the figure in the sample problem below.

Sample

▶ The figure below is composed of two rectangles and two triangles joined together.

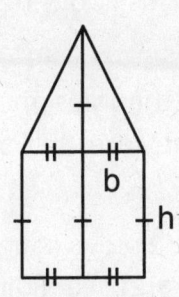

What is true of the four shapes?

A. All of the legs are congruent.

B. The height of the triangles is congruent to the height of the rectangles.

C. The base of the triangles are **not** congruent to the base of the rectangles.

D. The area of the triangles is the same as the area of the rectangles.

Lesson 6: Similarity and Congruence

How to Answer

Step 1 Read the question carefully. You are asked arrive at a logical deduction, based on your knowledge of congruency.

Step 2 Remember that congruent line segments are denoted with the same number of marks. You might plug values into the base and height of the figures to help you see which of the answer choices is true.

Step 3 Notice that the figure is made up of 2 rectangles and 2 triangles. From the diagram and your understanding of congruency, you can determine that the height, h, of the rectangles is the same as the height of the triangles. Additionally, you can tell that the base, b, of the triangles is the same as the width of the rectangles. The markings on the line segments tell you this.

Step 4 Read all the answer choices and use Process of Elimination to find the correct answer.

Answer choice **A** says that all of the legs are congruent. In Step 3, you noted that the heights of the triangles and the rectangles are the same. You also noted that the base of the triangles and the rectangles are the same. But the heights and the bases are not the same value, as shown in the diagram by the single mark in the heights and the double has mark in the bases. This answer choice isn't correct. Eliminate it.

Answer choice **B** says that the heights of the triangles and the rectangles are congruent. You found that to be true. This could be the correct answer. Check the other choices to be sure.

Answer choice **C** says that the bases of the triangles and rectangles are **not** congruent. The markings prove that they are, so you can eliminate this answer choice.

Answer choice **D** says that the area of the triangles is the same as the area of the rectangles. Plug in some values and see. For example, you can make the height 8 inches and the base 4 inches. The area of the rectangles would be $2bh = 2(4 \text{ inches})(8 \text{ inches}) = 64 \text{ inches}^2$. The area of the triangles would be $bh = (4 \text{ inches})(8 \text{ inches}) = 32 \text{ inches}^2$. They're not the same. Answer choice **B** is correct.

Step 5 You determined that answer choice **B** is correct. On the actual OGT, you would carefully fill in the bubble for **B** in your answer document.

Tip!

If two figures in a composite figure share an edge, it means that the measure of the edge is equal for both figures. This knowledge can help you determine congruency, as well as to find the area or volume of a composite figure.

Now You Try It!

1. The figure below is formed by 2 triangles and a rectangle.

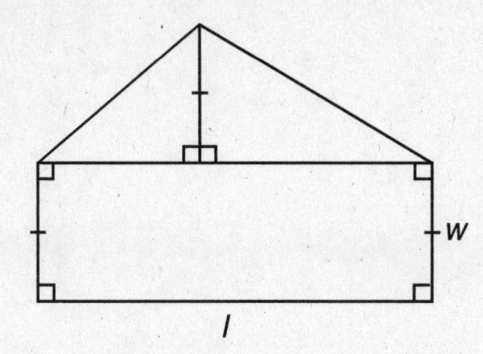

   What do the 3 shapes have in common?

   A. The height of the triangles and the width of the rectangle are congruent.

   B. The 3 shapes each have equal areas.

   C. The bases of both triangles are congruent.

   D. The volume of the 2 triangles is equal to the volume of the rectangle.

Lesson 6: Similarity and Congruence

2. Two similar triangles are drawn below.

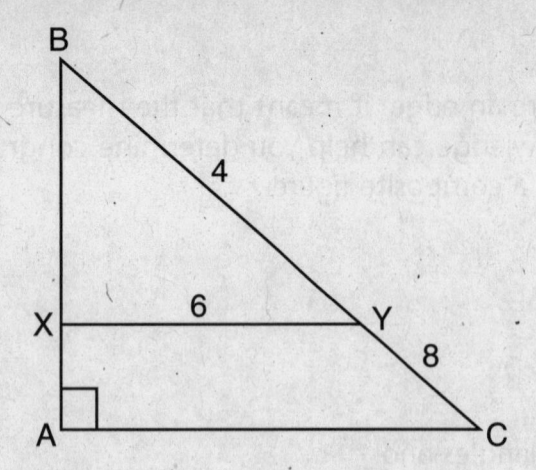

What is the measure of line segment $\overline{AC}$?

A. 8
B. 10
C. 12
D. 18

3. Triangles ABC and DEC are shown in the diagram below. Angles A and D <u>are</u> right angles and C is the midpoint of $\overline{AD}$.

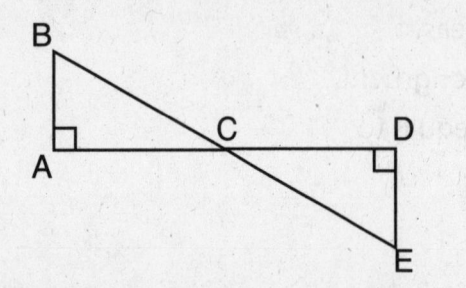

If the triangles are congruent, what statement is true about them?

A. $\overline{AB} \cong \overline{CE}$
B. $\angle DCE \cong \angle BCA$
C. $\angle ABC \cong \angle DCE$
D. $\overline{BC} \cong \overline{DE}$

4. Letitia has two fish tanks that are rectangular in shape. The bigger tank has a length of 24 inches and a width of 18 inches. The smaller one is proportional in shape and has a length of 8 inches.

   What should be the width of the smaller tank?
   A. 6 inches
   B. 8 inches
   C. 10 inches
   D. 12 inches

5. Brent thinks that the two triangles below look alike. He decides to measure the angles to see if they are congruent.

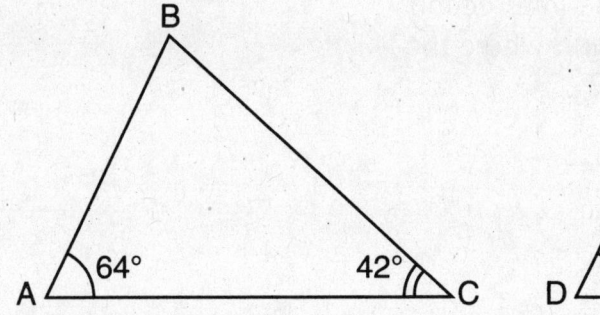

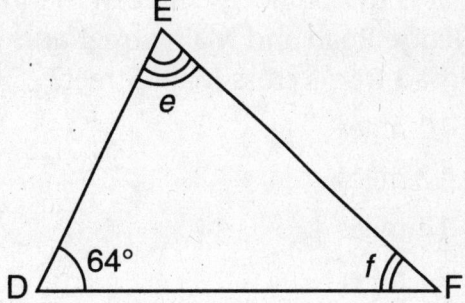

   What should be the measure of angle e if the triangles are congruent?
   A. 42
   B. 64
   C. 74
   D. 106

Lesson 6: Similarity and Congruence

6. The map below shows a section of a city street. High Road, State Street, and Main Street are parallel. Ridge Road is perpendicular to the three parallel streets.

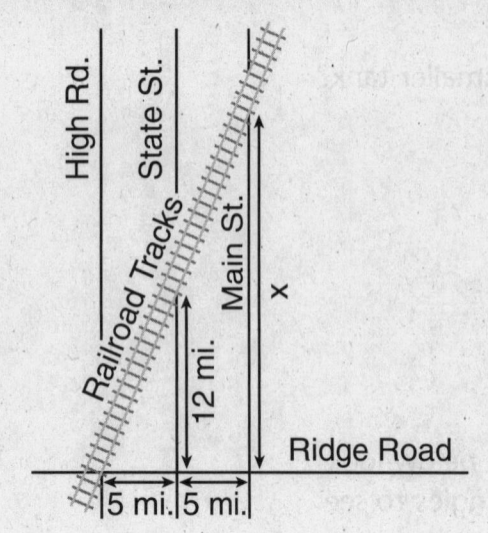

What is the distance between the intersection of Ridge Road and Main Street and where the railroad tracks cross Main Street?

A. 10 miles
B. 12 miles
C. 18 miles
D. 24 miles

7. Beryl knows that the two triangles below are similar.

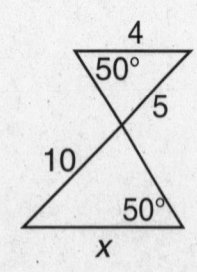

What is the length of x?

A. 4
B. 6
C. 8
D. 10

60 Roadmap to the Ohio Graduation Test: Mathematics

LESSON 7
GEOMETRIC FIGURES AND COORDINATE GRIDS

> GEOMETRY AND SPATIAL SENSE A, D, E, AND G

About This Benchmark

You will be locating the missing coordinates of figures like quadrilaterals and triangles drawn on a coordinate grid. You will be using 3-dimensional figures for some problem solving. You will also have to use the distance formula and determine the slope of a line to answer some questions.

VOCABULARY REVIEW

A **polygon** is a closed two-dimensional figure with straight sides.

A **quadrilateral** is a polygon with four angles and four sides. Squares, parallelograms, trapezoids, rhombuses, kites, and rectangles are examples of quadrilaterals.

A **triangle** is a polygon with three angles and three sides.

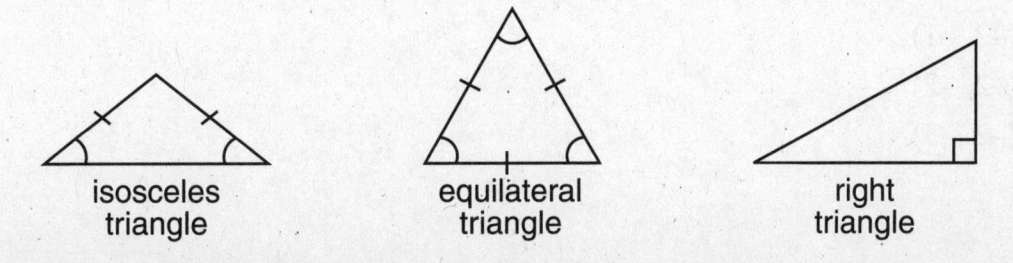

isosceles triangle

equilateral triangle

right triangle

Lesson 7: Geometric Figures and Coordinate Grids

61

Coordinates are numbers in an ordered pair; for example (x, y). The first number in the ordered pair is the x-coordinate. The second number is the y-coordinate. These numbers tell you where to locate a point on a coordinate grid.

A **coordinate grid** is a plane in which a horizontal number line intersects a vertical number line at their zero points.

The **slope** of a line is the ratio of the change in the y-coordinates, or the rise, to the corresponding change in the x-coordinates, or the run. The slope of a line is found with the formula $m = \frac{y_2 - y_1}{x_2 - x_1}$.

The **distance formula** is used to find the distance between two points on the coordinate plane. The formula is $d = \sqrt{(x_2 - x_1)^2 + (y_2 - y_1)^2}$.

Sample

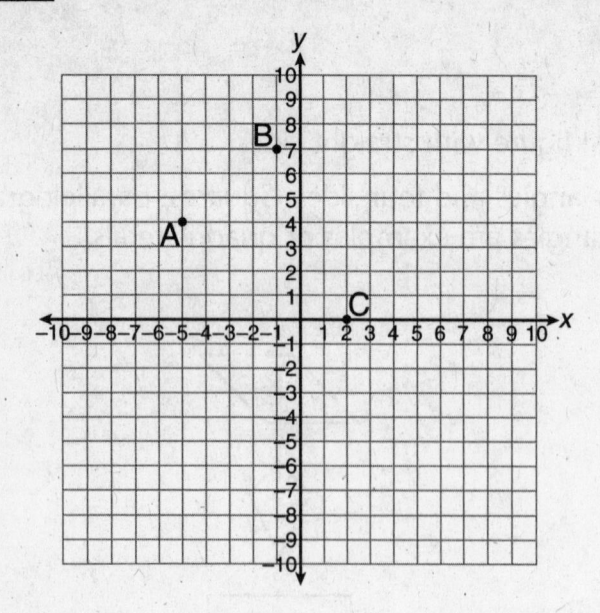

▶ Points A, B, and C are three vertices of a parallelogram. What are the coordinates of the fourth vertex of parallelogram ABCD?

A. (–2, 0)
B. (–2, –1)
C. (–2, –2)
D. (–2, –3)

How to Answer

Step 1 Carefully read the question. The coordinate grid is showing three points of a parallelogram. You are asked to find the point that will complete the figure.

Step 2 You may want to draw a parallelogram to help you answer the question.

Step 3 There are two ways you can find the other point. One way is to count the units from point B to point C and using that answer to count from point A to find point D. Another way to do it is to count the units from point B to point A and then use that answer to count the units from then you can use the other method to check your answer.

To get from point B to point A, go down 3 units and then to the left 4 units. To find point D, go down 3 units from point C and to the left 4 units. You should find point D at coordinates (−2, −3).

Step 4 Check your answer. Use the other method to see if you get the same answer. Count the units from point B to point C. Go down 7 units and to the right 3 units. Now, use the same count to go from point A to find point D. You should end up in the exact same spot as Step 3, (−2, −3). You've found the same answer with two different methods, so it must be right. The other way to check is to make sure that when the points are connected, the figure is a parallelogram.

Step 5 Read all of the answer choices. The *x*-coordinate in all of the answer choices matches your answer. Look at the *y*-coordinate. The only answer choice with a *y*-coordinate of −3 is answer choice **D**. This must be the correct answer.

Step 6 You determined that answer choice **D** is correct. On the actual OGT, you should carefully fill in the appropriate bubble on your answer document, making sure that you are filling in the space for the correct question number and the correct answer choice.

Lesson 7: Geometric Figures and Coordinate Grids

> **Tip!**

When you are placing points on a coordinate grid, make sure that you are careful about which coordinate point is the *x*-coordinate and which coordinate point is the *y*-coordinate. Always remember that the *x*-coordinate comes before the *y*-coordinate. (It may help to remember this rhyme: "x before y; walk before you fly.")

> **Now You Try It!**

1. Sarafina cut out the shape below from cardboard.

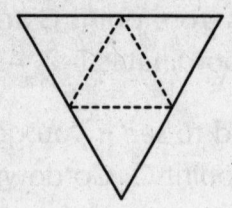

    When Sarafina folds the cardboard, what shape will she get?

    A. triangular prism
    B. triangular pyramid
    C. cone
    D. rectangular pyramid

2. Petra cut off the bottom of an object as shown below.

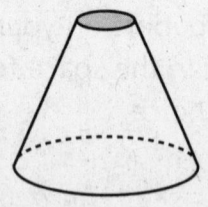

    What three-dimensional figure has Petra cut off from the existing figure?

    A. cylinder
    B. triangular pyramid
    C. cone
    D. rectangular pyramid

3.

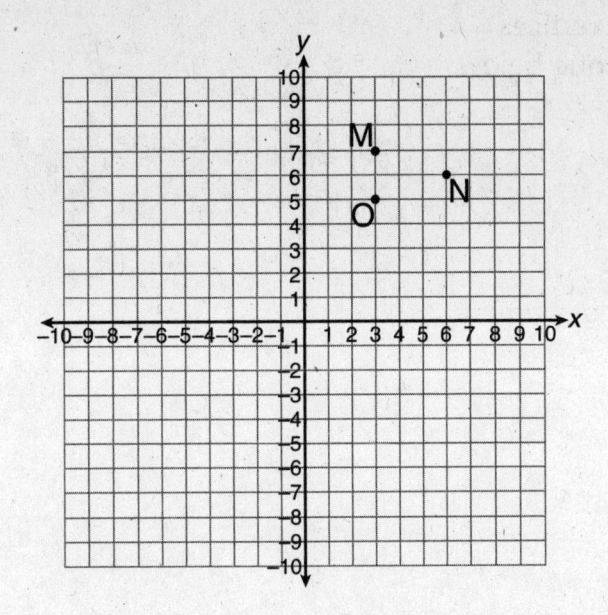

Points M, N, and O are three vertices of a kite with congruent sides. The kite is shaped like a parallelogram. What are the coordinates of the fourth vertex of kite MNOP?

A. (−1, 5)
B. (0, 6)
C. (1, 5)
D. (1, 6)

4. Michael cut off a corner of a box as illustrated below.

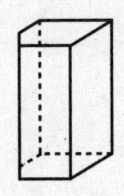

What type of three-dimensional figure has been cut off?

A. triangular prism
B. rectangular prism
C. rectangular pyramid
D. triangular pyramid

Lesson 7: Geometric Figures and Coordinate Grids

5. Marion counted the faces and vertices of a rectangular prism like the one below.

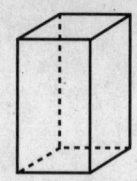

   How many faces and vertices does the figure have?

   A. 4 faces, 6 vertices

   B. 5 faces, 6 vertices

   C. 6 faces, 8 vertices

   D. 8 faces, 8 vertices

6. Two points are connected with a line on the following coordinate plane.

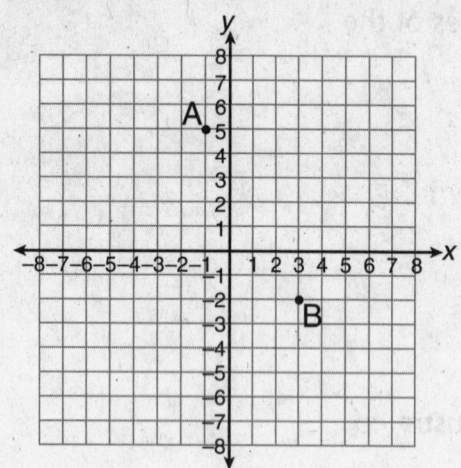

   Find the slope of line $\overline{AB}$.

   A. $-\frac{3}{4}$

   B. $-\frac{7}{4}$

   C. $\frac{3}{4}$

   D. $\frac{7}{4}$

7. A line is sketched on the coordinate plane with the endpoints at (–3, 8) and (5, 4). What is the distance between the two points?

   A. $\sqrt{28}$

   B. $\sqrt{62}$

   C. $\sqrt{80}$

   D. $\sqrt{148}$

8. The endpoints of $\overline{PQ}$ are P(–3, 0) and Q(3, 8). Find the slope of the line.

   A. $\frac{3}{4}$

   B. $\frac{4}{3}$

   C. 0

   D. 8

Lesson 7: Geometric Figures and Coordinate Grids

9. A circle on the coordinate plane has its center at (–2, –3). The circle passes through the point (3, 1). Which of these expressions could be used to find the radius, r, of the circle?

A. $\sqrt{(3-2)^2 + (1-3)^2}$

B. $\sqrt{(3+2)^2 + (1-3)^2}$

C. $\sqrt{(3-2)^2 + (1+3)^2}$

D. $\sqrt{(3+2)^2 + (1+3)^2}$

LESSON 8
ANGLES AND LINES

GEOMETRY AND SPATIAL SENSE C

About This Benchmark

You will be solving problems with complementary and supplementary angles. Some questions on the OGT may ask you about vertical angles, and others may ask about the angles formed by the intersection of a transversal.

VOCABULARY REVIEW

Parallel lines do not and will never meet or cross each other.

Perpendicular lines form 90° angles where they intersect.

Complementary angles are two angles that, when added together, measure 90°.

Supplementary angles are two angles that, when added together, measure 180°.

Vertical angles are two angles that are diagonally opposite each other when two lines intersect. Vertical angles are always equal to each other.

Two lines intersected by a third line, called a **transversal**, form 8 angles. Various pairs of these angles have special names.

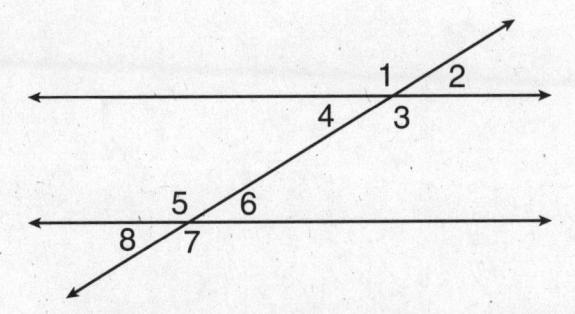

- In the diagram above, angles 3 and 6 are called **same-side interior angles**, as are angles 4 and 5.
- In the diagram above, angles 3 and 5 are called **alternate interior angles**, as are angles 4 and 6.
- In the diagram above, angles 1 and 5 are called **corresponding angles**, as are angles 2 and 6, 3 and 7, and 4 and 8.

Sample

▶ The diagram of triangle ABC is shown below.

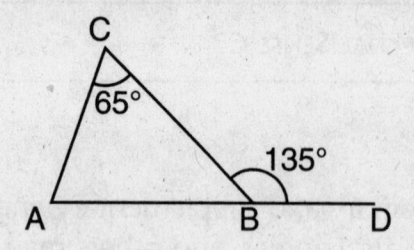

```
      C
     /|
    /65°
   /  \
  /    \___135°
 /_____
A        B       D
```

What is the measure of ∠CAB?

A. 45°
B. 70°
C. 115°
D. 230°

How to Answer

Step 1 Read the question carefully and make sure that you know what it is asking. You may have underlined ∠CAB or circled that angle in your booklet.

Step 2 You might want to recall at the definition of a supplementary angle to begin to solve the problem.

Step 3 The diagram shows you that ∠CBD is 135°. Because ∠CBD and ∠CBA are supplementary and equal 180° when added together, ∠CBA must be 45°. 180 − 135 = 45. Next, you know that the sum of the angles of a triangle equals 180°. Add ∠ACB and ∠CBA to get 65 + 45 = 110. ∠CAB must equal 70°. 180 − 110 = 70.

Step 4 Check your answer by going through the calculations again. Or you can work the problem backward by adding the value of the supplementary angles: 135 + 45 = 180, so that's right. Then, find the sum of the 3 angles of the triangle: 65 + 45 + 70 = 180. That works, which means you likely found the correct answer.

Step 5 Read all the answer choices. Answer choice **A** is the measure of one of the supplementary angles and isn't correct. Draw a line through it. Answer choice **B** matches your answer and looks right. Check the others to be sure. Answer choice **C** is 115° and if it was added to the given angle of 65°, you would have two angles that equal 180°, and that's impossible. Draw a line through it. Answer choice **D** is larger than the sum of three angles of a triangle and can be eliminated.

Step 6 You determined that answer choice **B** is correct. You would fill in the appropriate bubble on your answer document, making sure that you are filling in the space for the correct question number and the correct answer choice.

Tip!

Before solving a problem about the measure of an angle, be careful to know if you're working with angles that will add up to 90° or 180°.

Sometimes you'll find that it's the measure of an angle on the opposite side of a figure that will help you solve a problem. Don't expect to always find the angle that will help you to be right next to a missing measure.

Lesson 8: Angles and Lines

1. In the diagram below, $\overline{AB}$ is parallel to $\overline{CD}$.

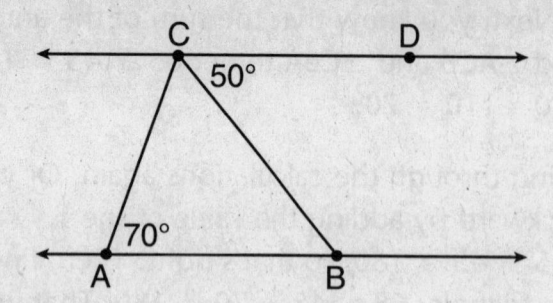

   What is the measure of ∠ACB?
   A. 40°
   B. 50°
   C. 60°
   D. 90°

2. Two lines intersect in the figure below and m∠3 = 6t + 30, m∠2 = 8t − 60.

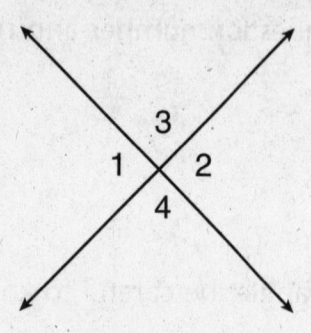

   What is the measure of ∠4?
   A. 45°
   B. 60°
   C. 120°
   D. 140°

3. Main Street and Avenue A are parallel to each other, and they are intersected by 52nd Street and Surf Road, as shown below. ∠b = 44° and ∠c = 51°.

What is the measure of ∠a?

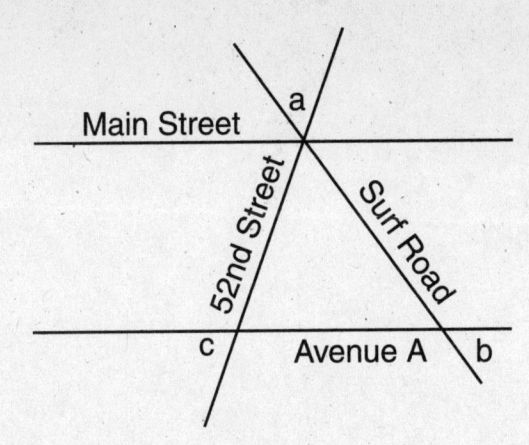

A. 83°
B. 85°
C. 95°
D. 97°

4. Parallel lines $\overline{AB}$ and $\overline{CD}$ are intersected by transversal $\overline{EF}$ at points X and Y as below.

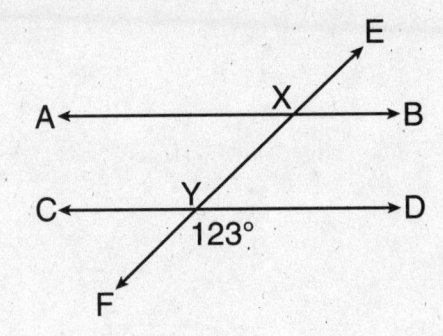

What is the measure of ∠AXE?

A. 29°
B. 51°
C. 75°
D. 123°

Lesson 8: Angles and Lines

5. Triangle ABC is shown in the diagram below.

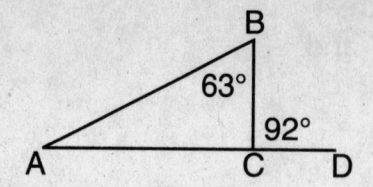

   What is the measure of ∠BAC?
   A. 29°
   B. 51°
   C. 63°
   D. 88°

6. The right triangle BEC with straight line $\overrightarrow{AD}$ is shown in the diagram below.

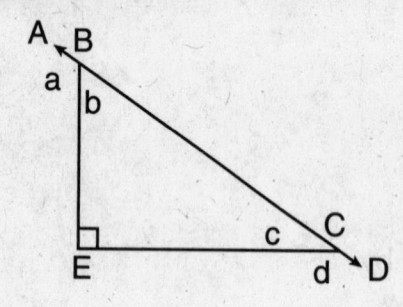

   What does a° + d° equal?
   A. 135°
   B. 160°
   C. 180°
   D. 270°

LESSON 9
TRANSFORMATIONS

GEOMETRY AND SPATIAL SENSE F

About This Benchmark
You will practice identifying the three types of transformations: translations, reflections, and rotations. Some questions on the OGT may ask you to predict the results of a transformation.

VOCABULARY REVIEW

A **transformation** is the movement of a figure from one position to another position.

A **translation** is a type of transformation in which a figure is moved horizontally or vertically—or both.

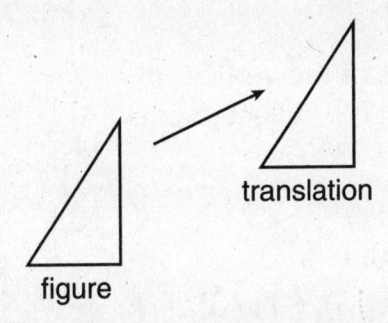

A **reflection** is a type of transformation in which a figure is flipped over a line.

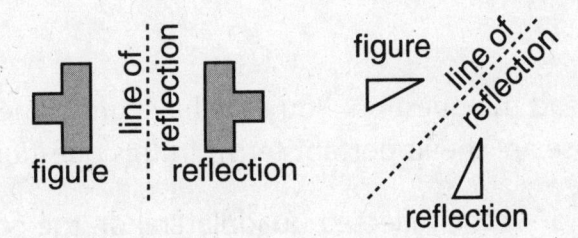

A **rotation** is a type of transformation where a figure is moved around a fixed point.

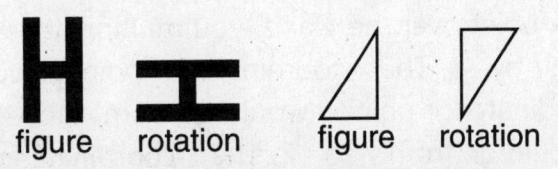

Lesson 9: Transformations

75

Multiple-Choice Sample

▶ The quadrilateral ABCD has vertices at the coordinates (3, 3), (4, 5), (7, 5), and (8, 3), as shown.

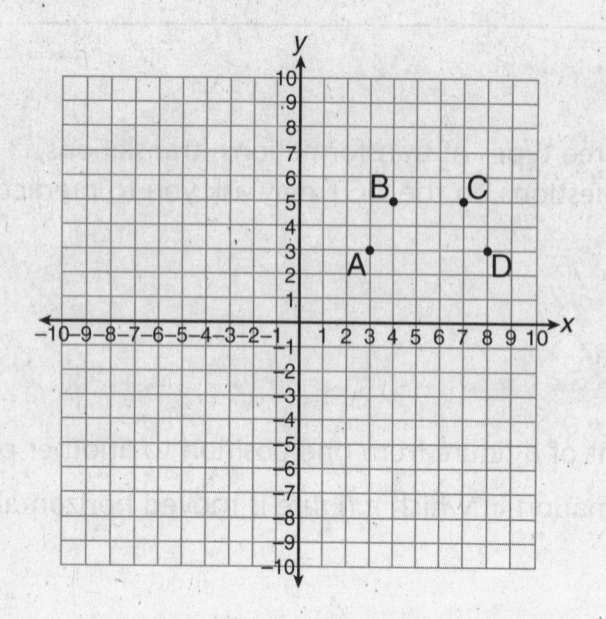

What are the coordinates of the vertices of quadrilateral ABCD when it is reflected over the y-axis?

A. (3, 3), (4, 5), (7, 5), (8, 3)
B. (−3, 3), (−4, 5), (−7, 5), (−8, 3)
C. (−3, −3), (−4, −5), (−7, −5), (−8, −3)
D. (3, −3), (4, −5), (7, −5), (8, −3)

How to Answer

Step 1 Carefully read the question. You may have underlined *reflected* and *y*-axis. Those are the important terms in this question.

Step 2 You might draw the reflected quadrilateral on the coordinate grid. Be sure not to confuse the *x*- and *y*-axes.

Step 3 To reflect a point over the *y*-axis, you multiply the *x*-coordinate of each ordered pair by −1. The *x*-coordinate for point A would go from 3 to −3. The *x*-coordinate for point B would go from 4 to −4. The *x*-coordinate for point C would go from 7 to −7. The *x*-coordinate for D would go from 8 to −8. The *y*-coordinates for each ordered pair would remain the same.

Step 4 Check your answer. Make sure that it is the x-coordinate of each point that you have multiplied by –1. If you drew a reflected quadrilateral over the y-axis, is it similar to the original quadrilateral? If the shape looks noticeably different, you likely plotted a point incorrectly.

Step 5 Read all of the answer choices. The coordinates listed in answer choice **A** is the same as the coordinates of the quadrilateral given in the question so it's not right. Draw a line through answer choice **A**. Answer choice **B** looks like the right answer because it lists the same coordinates from Step 3. As always, check the other answer choices to be sure. In answer choice **C**, both the x- and y-coordinates have been multiplied by –1. That's not right, so draw a line through it. The y-coordinate in answer choice **D** has been multiplied by –1, which would reflect the quadrilateral over the x-axis. Cross that choice out as well.

Step 6 You have found that answer choice **B** is correct. On the OGT, you would fill in the appropriate bubble on your answer document.

Extended-Response Sample

▶ Triangle PQR has vertices with coordinates P(–7, 2), Q(–4, 2), and R(–4, –3).

Draw and label triangle PQR on the grid below. (On the actual OGT, the grid will be in your separate **answer document**.)

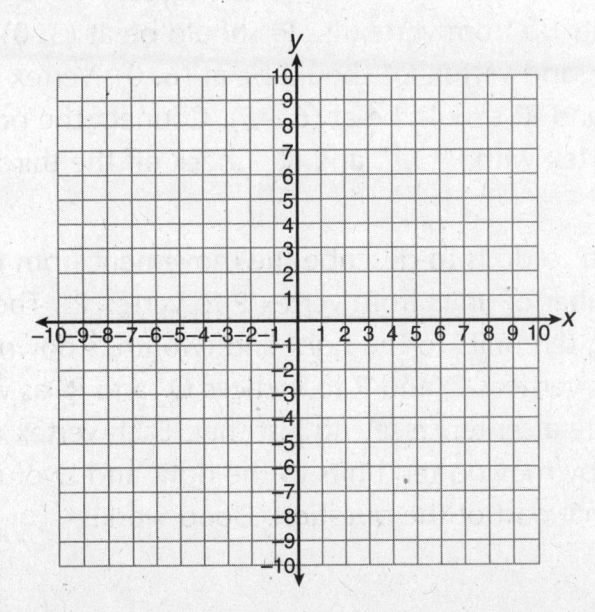

Lesson 9: Transformations

Draw triangle P'Q'R' by translating all three vertices of triangle PQR five units to the right and then five units down. Label triangle P'Q'R'.

Draw triangle P"Q"R" by translating all three vertices of triangle P'Q'R' five units to the right and then three units up. Label triangle P"Q"R".

What movements do you need to perform a single translation of each vertex from triangle PQR to triangle P"Q"R"?

How to Answer

Step 1 Read the question carefully. The question is asking you to draw the original plus two translated triangles and then to describe the movement from the original triangle to the third triangle.

Step 2 There are four parts in this question, so you may want to check off each part as you complete it.

Step 3 First, use the given coordinates to draw triangle PQR on the grid provided. Check off the first part of the question.

Next, you want to draw triangle P'Q'R', so start at vertex P and count five units to the right and five units down. Vertex P should go from $(-7, 2)$ to P' at $(-2, -3)$. Do the same with vertex Q at $(-4, 2)$ and you should find Q' at $(1, -3)$. Vertex R at $(-4, -3)$ should become vertex R' at $(1, -8)$. Connect the points and label each new vertex with P', Q', and R'. Check off the second part of the question.

Now you want to draw triangle P"Q"R". For vertex P', count five units to the right and three units up from vertex P'. P" should be at $(3, 0)$. Do the same with point Q' and vertex Q" should be at $(6, 0)$. Vertex R' is moved the same way and R" should be at $(6, -5)$. Connect the points and label each new vertex with P", Q", and R". Check off the third part of the question.

The last thing you need to do is to describe the movement from PQR to P"Q"R". Count the number of units from vertex P to vertex P". The vertex is translated by moving ten units to the right and two units down. (That should be the same for vertices Q and R to vertices Q" and R" as well.) You would need to write a sentence saying just that: Each vertex of PQR is translated to P"Q"R" by moving ten units to the right and two units down. Check off the final part of the question. Good work!

Step 4 Check your answer. Read through the problem again and count each translation to make sure you have moved the vertices correctly. Your grid should look like the diagram below.

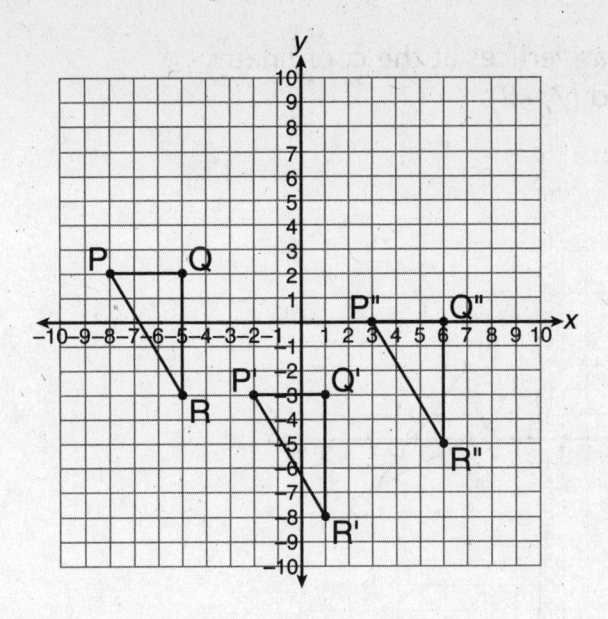

Step 5 Make sure that your drawings and your written answer are clear and easy to read.

Tip!

Use your experience in the real world to help you understand transformations. For example, you see a reflection in a mirror. The mirror creates a reflection in the same way that the x- or y-axis can create a reflection. When you rotate, you turn your body and face in another direction. The same rule applies with a geometric figure! When a figure rotates, it changes its direction as well.

Lesson 9: Transformations

Now You Try It!

1. Triangle MNO has vertices at the coordinates (3, 0), (3, 3), and (7, −2).

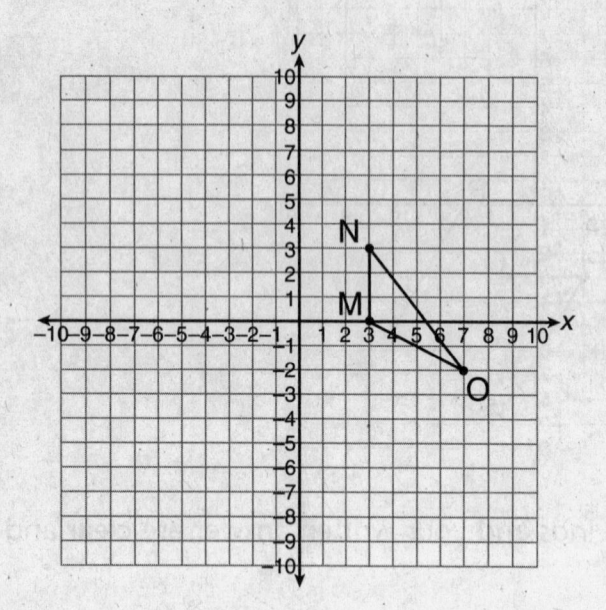

   What are the coordinates of the vertices of triangle MNO when it is reflected over the x-axis?

   A. (3, 0), (3, 3), (7, −2)
   B. (−3, 0), (−3, 3), (−7, −2)
   C. (−3, 0), (−3, −3), (−7, 2)
   D. (3, 0), (3, −3), (7, 2)

2. Quadrilateral WXYZ has vertices at coordinates (–8, –3), (–5, –3), (–2, –7), and (–9, –7).

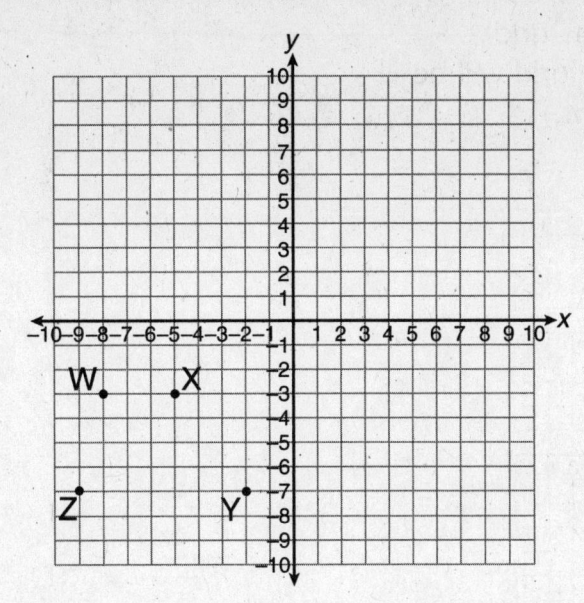

If WXYZ is translated six units to the right and nine units up, what are the coordinates of the vertices of the new quadrilateral?

A. (–2, 6), (1, 6), (4, 2), (–3, –2)
B. (–2, 5), (1, 5), (4, 1), (–3, –1)
C. (–3, 6), (0, 6), (3, 2), (–2, –2)
D. (–3, 5), (0, 5), (3, 1), (–2, –1)

Lesson 9: Transformations

3. The triangle KLM has vertices with the coordinates K(5, 8), L(7, 3), and M(2, 4).

   Draw and label triangle KLM on the grid provided. (On the actual OGT, the grid will be in your separate **answer document**.)

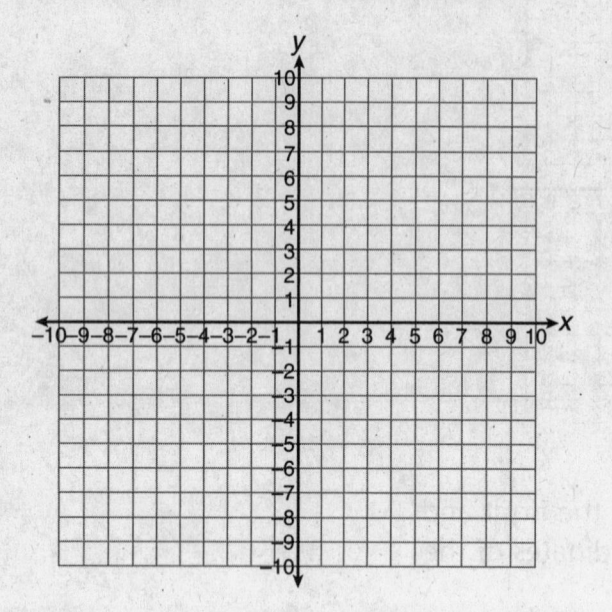

   Draw triangle K'L'M' by translating each vertex of KLM four units to the left and also five units down. Label triangle K'L'M'.

   Draw triangle K"L"M" by translating each vertex of K'L'M' six units to the left and also three units up. Label triangle K"L"M".

   What movements are needed to perform a single translation of the three vertices from triangle KLM to triangle K"L"M"?

LESSON 10
PATTERNS AND SEQUENCES

> PATTERNS, FUNCTIONS, AND ALGEBRA A

About This Benchmark

You will practice understanding various types of patterns. You will also identify and solve problems with arithmetic and geometric sequences.

VOCABULARY REVIEW

A **pattern** is a series of numbers or shapes that follows a rule.

A **sequence** is a series of numbers in a certain order.

An **arithmetic sequence** is a sequence formed by adding the same number to the previous term or subtracting the same number from the previous term.

A **geometric sequence** is a sequence formed by multiplying the previous term by the same number or dividing the previous term by the same number.

A **formula** for the nth term of a sequence is a way to define the sequence. That is, instead of listing all the terms in the sequence, it is more concise to create a formula that tells you what the nth term will be when you plug in the value for n. For example, the sequence –2, 3, –4, –5, –6, . . . can be written as $(-1)^n(n + 1)$ for $n \geq 1$. So if you wanted to know the 100th term, you could plug 100 into the formula to get 101.

Lesson 10: Patterns and Sequences

Sample

▶ The first four terms of a pattern are shown below.

○   ○○   ○○○   ○○○○
      ○○   ○○○   ○○○○
            ○○○   ○○○○
                     ○○○○

Assuming the pattern shown above continues, what would be the fifth term?

A.
○○○○
○○○○
○○○○
○○○○

B.
○○○○
○○○○
○○○○
○○○○
○○○○

C.
○○○○○
○○○○○
○○○○○
○○○○○
○○○○○

D.
○○○○○○
○○○○○○
○○○○○○
○○○○○○
○○○○○○
○○○○○○

How to Answer

Step 1   Carefully read the question. You are looking for the next term in the pattern.

Step 2   You might choose to draw the fifth term in the geometric pattern.

Step 3 First, you need to identify the pattern. Count the number of circles in each term, 1, 4, 9, and 16. You could use an equation to find the fifth term because each term is a square of that term. The first is $1^2 = 1$, the second is $2^2 = 4$, the third is $3^2 = 9$, and the fourth is $4^2 = 16$. That means the fifth term is $5^2 = 25$.

Step 4 Check your answer. When you look at the circles in the question stem, you see that the second term has 2 circles across and 2 down; the third term has 3 circle across and 3 down; and the fourth term has 4 circles across and 4 down. If you draw the fifth term, you would have 5 circles across and 5 circles down, or 25 circles. This is the same answer as Step 3.

Step 5 Now look at each answer choice. You can eliminate answer choices **A**, **B**, and **D** because they don't have 25 circles. Answer choice **C** is correct.

Step 6 You would fill in the bubble for answer choice **C** on your answer document.

Tip!

Once you think you have found the pattern or determined the rule for a sequence, test it against every term in the pattern or sequence. If it doesn't work for every term, it isn't right.

Now You Try It!

1. Allison places a bacterium in a dish that doubles in volume every 5 minutes. The dish is full 2 hours after Allison places the bacterium in the dish.

   How full is the dish 90 minutes after Allison placed the bacterium in the dish?

   A. $\frac{3}{4}$ full

   B. $\frac{1}{16}$ full

   C. $\frac{1}{32}$ full

   D. $\frac{1}{64}$ full

Lesson 10: Patterns and Sequences

2. The figure below shows the first three stages of a method of piling cannonballs.

    Stage 1   Stage 2   Stage 3

   Assuming the pattern continues, how many cannonballs will be in Stage 6?

   A. 10
   B. 15
   C. 21
   D. 28

3. The clover honey farm gets 5 pounds of honey from 2 hives. They get 12.5 pounds of honey from 5 hives, 22.5 pounds of honey from 9 hives, and 30 pounds of honey from 12 hives.

   How many pounds of honey could the clover honey farm expect to yield from 21 hives?

   A. 50 pounds
   B. 52.5 pounds
   C. 55 pounds
   D. 57.5 pounds

4. The pattern below continues indefinitely.

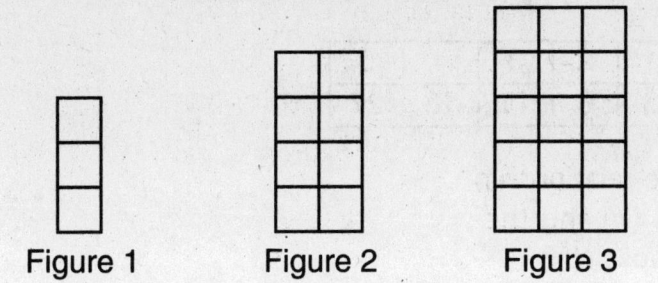

Figure 1   Figure 2   Figure 3

How many squares will make up Figure 8?

A. 50
B. 60
C. 70
D. 80

5. Benny is gathering pinecones for his mother. He figured he could get 42 pinecones from 3 trees, 70 pinecones from 5 trees, and 112 pinecones from 8 trees.

If Benny continued this collection process, how many trees would it take him to gather 280 pinecones?

A. 10
B. 15
C. 20
D. 28

Lesson 10: Patterns and Sequences   **87**

6. The table below contains the results of a used book drive by the library.

Day (n)	1	2	3	4	5
Number of Books (b)	3	6	11	18	27

Which of these represents the relationship between the number of Days (n) and the corresponding Number of Books (b)?

A. $b = n^2 + 2$
B. $b = 2^n$
C. $b = 2n + 2$
D. $b = 2n^2 - 2$

7. The sequence of letters below forms a pattern.

    B X D W F V H U

If the pattern continues, what would be the next letter in the sequence?

A. J
B. B
C. T
D. G

LESSON 11
FUNCTIONS AND EQUATIONS

> PATTERNS, FUNCTIONS, AND ALGEBRA B, C, D, E, F, I AND J

About This Benchmark

These Ohio benchmarks require you to understand, identify, and classify functions. You will see how one value in a function can be dependent upon another value in the function. You will practice understanding the relationships of values from functions shown in tables and diagrams. You will also examine the graphing of linear functions on the coordinate plane.

VOCABULARY REVIEW

A **function** is a relation in which an input term is paired with a unique output term according to a rule.

An **independent quantity** is the input of a function.

A **dependent quantity** is the output of a function. The dependent quantity *depends upon* the independent quantity.

An **equation** is a mathematical statement that uses an equal sign (=). The values on either side of the equal sign are equal to each other.

A **linear equation** is an equation that can be simplified such that its only terms are numbers, variables, and products of a number and a variable. For example, $y = 3x + 7$, $4i + 2 + 3x = 0$, $7y + 4i = 8$, $2x + 3z + 2y + 4 + 8 = 7z + 6$, and $2(4 + 5v) = 10$ are all examples of linear equations. A linear equation, when graphed, will create a straight line.

The *x*-intercept is the point at which the graph of a function crosses through the *x*-axis. For example, the *x*-intercept of the line $y = 2x + 4$ is (–2, 0). Because the *x*-intercept always lies on the *x*-axis, the *y*-coordinate is always 0.

The *y*-intercept is the point at which the graph of a function crosses through the *y*-axis. For example, the *y*-intercept of the line $y = 2x + 4$ is (0, 4). Because the *y*-intercept always lies on the *y*-axis, the *x*-coordinate is always 0.

The **slope-intercept form** of a linear equation is $y = mx + b$, where the slope is the coefficient of x. For example, the slope of the equation $y = \frac{2}{3}x + 4$ is $\frac{2}{3}$.

Parallel lines are lines that do not intersect. When graphed on a coordinate plane, parallel lines have the same slope.

Perpendicular lines are lines that intersect at right angles. When graphed on a coordinate plane, perpendicular lines will have slopes that are opposite reciprocals of each other, which means that their products equal –1.

Rate of change is the ratio of the change in the independent variable to the change in the dependent ratio. In the context of linear functions, the rate of change is the ratio of the change in y to the change in x, which is known as slope.

Sample

▶ Which equation represents the relationship between the x- and y-values shown in the table below?

x	y
−1	0.5
0	1
1	2
2	4
3	8

A. $y = 2^x$
B. $y = 2x$
C. $y = x + 2$
D. $y = x^2$

How to Answer

Step 1 Carefully read the question then look at the table. You will find that for every value of x, there is a value for y. In each case the value of y is determined by performing some mathematical operation on the value of x. You need to identify the equation that represents that relationship.

Step 2 One strategy you could use to answer this question is to look for a pattern. Each answer choice will produce a particular pattern between x and y. Try to determine the pattern that each answer choice will produce. Perhaps answer choice **A** is the most difficult because raising 2 to a negative power or to the zero power may not be an operation that you perform often. It may be easier to plug the values from the table into the equations in the answer choices to see which ones fit.

Step 3 Use Process of Elimination to eliminate the answer choices that you know are incorrect. Answer choice **B** would mean that doubling x will produce y. This rule is true for only two of the answer pairs, (1, 2) and (2, 4), from the table. Therefore, answer choice **B** cannot be the correct answer.

Answer choice **C** shows that each y will be 2 greater than the x-value. This rule is true only for (2, 4). It's not the case for the other pairs of values in the table. Therefore, answer choice **C** cannot be correct. Eliminate it from the list of possible choices.

Answer choice **D**, $y = x^2$, means that x times itself (in other words, x squared) will produce the value for y. From the table the only pair of numbers for which this rule is true is (2, 4) because 2 squared equals 4. You can conclude the answer choice **D** cannot be correct. Cross it off.

Step 4 Using POE, you have determined that answer choice **A** is likely the correct answer. Check this answer with the numbers in the table. Does $0.5 = 2^{-1}$? Does $1 = 2^0$? Does $2 = 2^1$? Does $4 = 2^2$? Does $8 = 2^3$? In each case the answer is yes, so answer choice **A** is indeed correct.

> **Tip!**

When a variable is multiplied by a number, the multiplication sign (×) is not usually used to show the multiplication. (The × looks very much like the variable x.) For example, to multiply the variable x by 2, the product can be written as 2x. You may also see the symbol •, which means the same thing as the multiplication symbol ×.

> **Now You Try It!**

1. Which graph below could represent the equation $4x - 3y = -6$?

A.

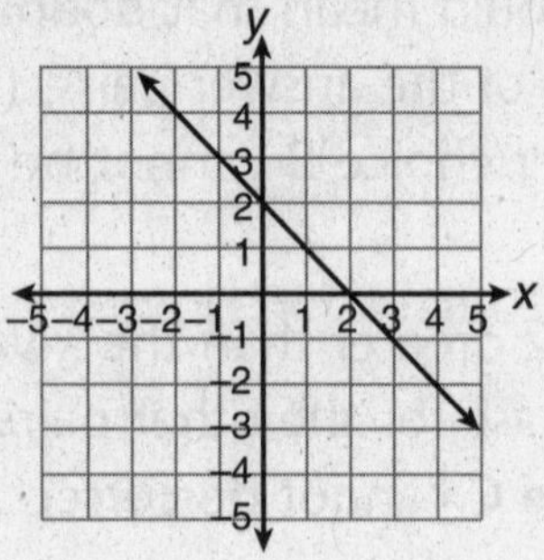

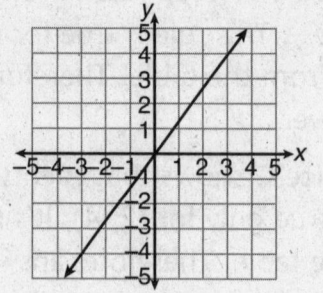

B.

C.

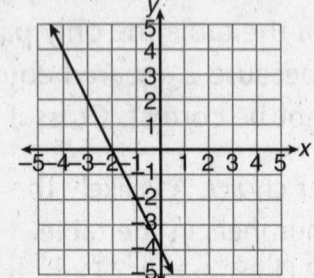

D.

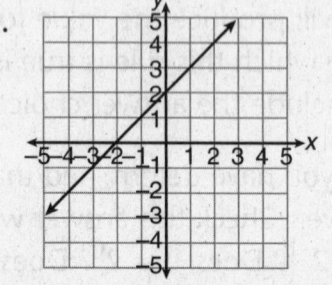

2. Which equation below is equivalent to $3(8x - 6) = 4(x - 5)$?

   A. $20x = -2$
   B. $20x = -38$
   C. $28x = 2$
   D. $28x = -38$

3. Luke calculates supplies he is going to buy with the following equation:

   $$2w + 8c = B$$

   B is Luke's total budget,
   w is the number of spools of wire, and
   c is the number of boxes of clay.

   Luke buys 4 boxes of clay. How many spools of wire will he be able to buy if his budget is $45?

   A. 5
   B. 6
   C. 7
   D. 8

4. Which pair of equations would represent two lines: the first that is perpendicular to the graph of $y = -6x + 8$ and the second that is parallel to the graph of $y = -6x + 8$?

   A. $y = -\frac{1}{6}x + 4$ and $y = -6x - \frac{1}{3}$
   B. $y = \frac{1}{6}x + 7$ and $y = -6x + 20$
   C. $y = 6x + 5$ and $y = -6x - \frac{1}{3}$
   D. $y = -6x + 9$ and $y = -6x + 20$

Lesson 11: Functions and Equations

5. The graph of the equation $9x + 6y = 24$ has which of the following points?

   A. (0, 2)
   B. (0, 3)
   C. (1, 1)
   D. (2, 1)

6. The graph below shows the daily high temperature for a city over a five-day period.

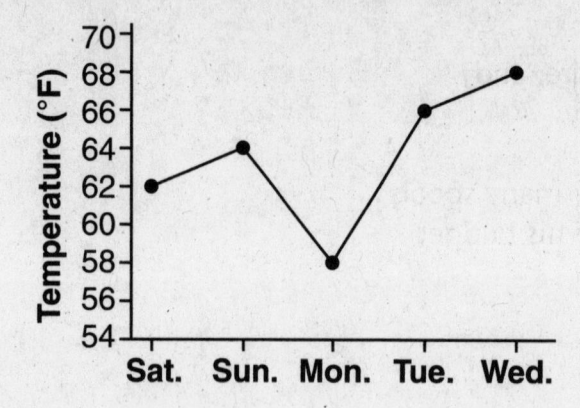

   Which day's high temperature increased the most compared to the previous day?

   A. Sunday
   B. Monday
   C. Tuesday
   D. Wednesday

7. Leonardo had a savings account with $95 in it. During the summer, he earned $200 a week, working on a farm. He deposited 80% of his earnings into his savings account each week.

   Which of these equations represents the amount of money, m, Leonardo will have deposited into his account after w weeks?

   A. $m = 25.5w$
   B. $m = 16w + 95$
   C. $m = 16w + 200$
   D. $m = 160w + 95$

8. Which equation represents the relationship between the x- and y-values shown in the table below?

x	y
0	2
1	1
2	0
3	−1
4	−2

   A. $y = x - 2$
   B. $y = 2x + 2$
   C. $y = -x + 2$
   D. $y = x + 2$

Lesson 11: Functions and Equations

9. A landscaping company uses the following equation to determine customers' bills:

$$B = 30h + 50$$

B equals the amount billed and
h is the number of hours the landscapers spent working on the customer's property.

How many hours will the landscapers spend working for the bill to be a total of $470?

A. 10
B. 12
C. 14
D. 16

10. Which of the equations is represented by the graph below?

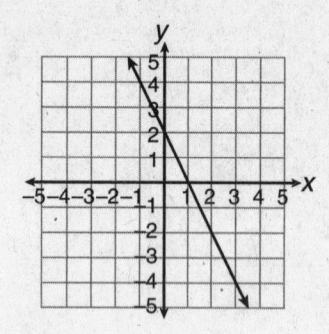

A. $-2x = y - 2$
B. $2x = y + 2$
C. $-3x = y - 1$
D. $3x = y + 1$

LESSON 12
INEQUALITIES

> PATTERNS, FUNCTIONS, AND ALGEBRA D AND F

About This Benchmark

You will be asked to solve problems with inequalities on the OGT. You will also need to demonstrate an understanding of graphs of inequalities.

VOCABULARY REVIEW

An **inequality** is a mathematical statement that uses $<$, $>$, $\neq$, $\leq$, or $\geq$. The values on either side of an inequality are generally not equal to each other.

Sample

▶ Gus received $250 for his birthday. He wants to use the money for fly fishing. The rod costs $95, the waders cost $80, and the lessons will cost $10 per hour.

Which inequality could Gus use to figure out the most hours, h, that he can take fly fishing lessons without spending more than $250?

A. $80 + 10h < 250$
B. $95 + 10h < 250$
C. $80 + 95 + 10h > 250$
D. $80 + 95 + 10h \leq 250$

How to Answer

Step 1 Carefully read the question. You are to find the inequality that will show how many hours Gus can take fly-fishing lessons, without exceeding his $250.

Step 2 You could try to write your own inequality that matches the information.

Lesson 12: Inequalities

Step 3 First, you might want to write the $250 with the inequality sign that fits the situation. Gus wants to spend *less than or equal* to $250, which is the ≤ sign. Write that part of the inequality: ≤ 250. Next, on the other side of the inequality, you'll want to add the costs that Gus will pay for: the rod is $95, the waders are $80, and the lessons are $10 per hour. That equals 95 + 80 + 10h. Now, put it all together to get 95 + 80 + 10h ≤ 250.

Step 4 Check your answer. Make sure that you've included all of the information that's been given to you in the question stem. You could solve the inequality to see if you get a reasonable answer: 95 + 80 + 10h ≤ 250 or 175 + 10h ≤ 250 or 10h ≤ 75 or h ≤ 7.5. That looks reasonable. Gus could take 7 hours of lessons and not exceed the $250.

Step 5 Read all of the answer choices. Answer choices **A** and **B** don't have the correct inequality sign. Answer choice **C** has the inequality sign in the wrong direction. That leaves answer choice **D**, which looks like the answer you got in Step 3.

Step 6 You determined that answer choice **D** is correct. So on the actual OGT you would fill in the appropriate bubble on your answer document, making sure that you are filling in the space for the correct question number and the correct answer choice.

Tip!

When the graph of an inequality has a dotted line, the sign is > or <. When the line is solid, the sign is ≤ or ≥.

Now You Try It!

1. Ruth is making bead necklaces from her collection of 829 beads. She uses small beads to make five 73-bead necklaces. She also makes *r* 48-bead necklaces and *s* 39-bead necklaces from the remaining beads.

   Which inequality describes this relationship?

   A. 5(73) + 48r + 39s ≤ 829

   B. (5 + r + s)(73 + 48 + 39) < 829

   C. 5(73) + 48r ≥ 829 − 39s

   D. 5(73) + (r + s)(48 + 39) ≤ 829

2. Which inequality is represented by the graph below?

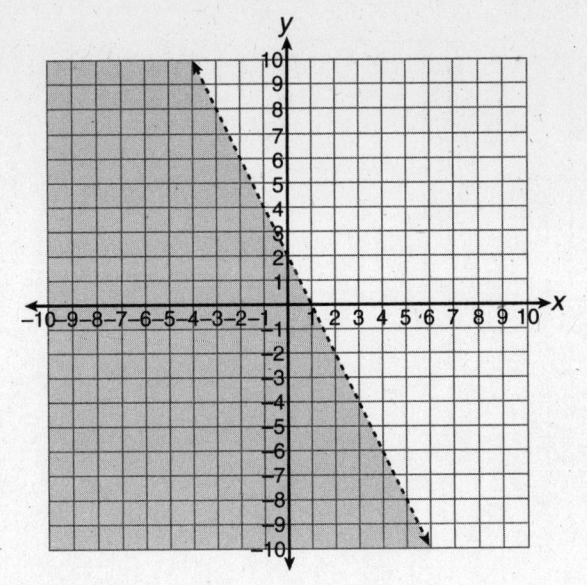

A. $y < -2x + 2$
B. $y > -2x + 2$
C. $x < -2y + 2$
D. $x > -2y + 2$

3. Jaime does not want to spend more than $40 on school supplies. Markers cost $6 each, pencils cost $1 each, and notebooks cost $2.50 each.

Which inequality would help Jaime to know how much can be spent on each item?

A. $6m + 2.5n \leq 40$
B. $6(m + p) + 2.5n < 40$
C. $6m + 1p + 2.5n \leq 40$
D. $6m \leq 40 - 2.5n$

Lesson 12: Inequalities

4. Which inequality is represented by the graph below?

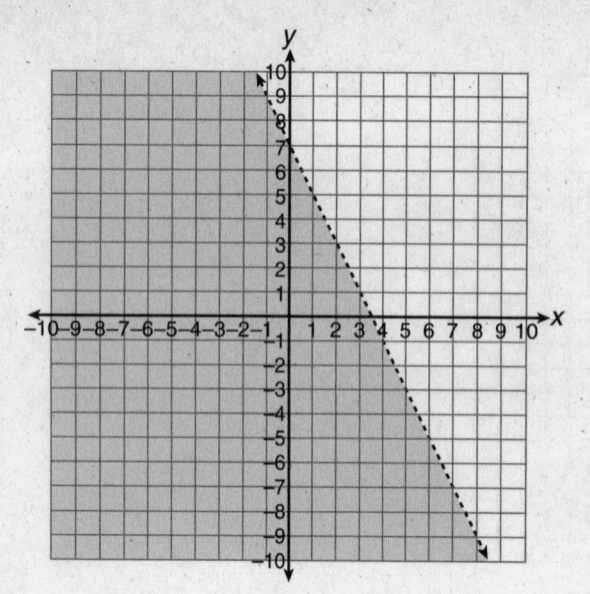

A. $2y + x < 7$
B. $2y + x \leq 7$
C. $2x + y < 7$
D. $2x + y \leq 7$

5. Sherri doesn't want to spend more than $50 in the next month and calculates her expenses with the following inequality:

$$2.5l + 7r < E$$

l is the number of school lunches she buys,
r is the riding lessons she takes, and
E is the total amount she wants to spend.

If Sherri buys 4 lunches, how many riding lessons will she be able to take?

A. 4
B. 5
C. 6
D. 7

6. Which inequality is represented by the graph below?

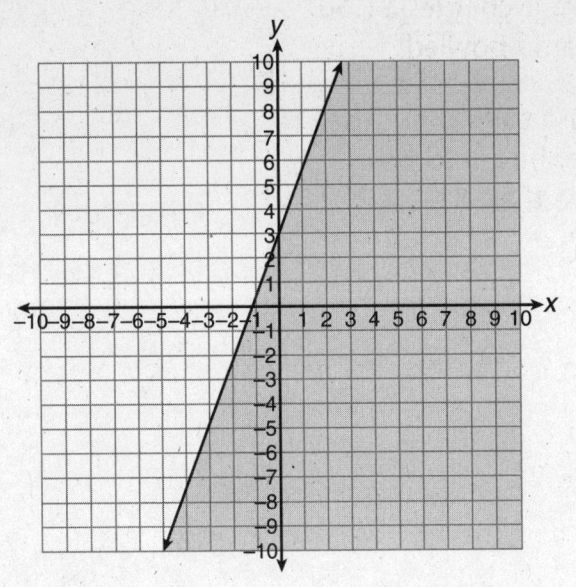

A. $y \leq 2x + 3$
B. $y > 2x + 3$
C. $y < 2x + 3$
D. $y \geq 2x + 3$

7. Taylor wants to buy new shirts and doesn't want to spend more than $125. The store where Taylor shops has 15% off on shirts that normally sell for $24.99.

Which inequality would Taylor use to determine the maximum number of shirts, s, he can buy during the sale?

A. $24.99s \times 0.85 < 125$
B. $(24.99 \times 0.85)s < 125$
C. $24.99s \times 0.85 \leq 125$
D. $(24.99 \times 0.85)s \leq 125$

Lesson 12: Inequalities

8. Alex went bowling with his friends after school. The bowling alley has a discount price for students from 4:00 to 6:00 p.m. It charges $1.50 to rent shoes, and $2.50 per game bowled.

   Which inequality should Alex use to find out the maximum number of games, g, he could bowl, if he didn't want to spend more than $11.50?

   A. $11.50 \geq 2.50g - 1.50$

   B. $2.50g + 1.50 \leq 11.50$

   C. $11.50 + 1.50 < 2.50g$

   D. $1.50g < 11.50 + 2.50$

9. Which inequality below is equivalent to $6(x + 9) > 4(3x - 2)$?

   A. $46 > 6x$

   B. $46 < 6x$

   C. $62 > 6x$

   D. $62 < 6x$

10. Which inequality below is equivalent to $2(3y - 7) \leq 8y + 4$?

    A. $-9 \leq y$

    B. $-28 \leq y$

    C. $-11 \leq 2y$

    D. $-28 \leq -2y$

LESSON 13
QUADRATIC EQUATIONS

PATTERNS, FUNCTIONS, AND ALGEBRA G

About This Benchmark

You will practice interpreting graphs of quadratic equations. Some questions on the OGT will not include a coordinate grid, but you can create your own grid to find a solution.

VOCABULARY REVIEW

A **quadratic equation** is an equation that contains at least one term that is a number multiplied by a variable raised to the second power and does not contain any terms with a variable raised to a power greater than two. If an equation can be rearranged to be in the form $ax^2 + bx + c = 0$, where $a \neq 0$, then it is a quadratic equation. A quadratic equation, when graphed, will create a **parabola**.

Sample

▶ What are the *x*-intercepts of the graph of the equation $y = x^2 - 5x + 6$?

A. $x = 5, x = 6$
B. $x = 6, x = -1$
C. $x = -2, x = -3$
D. $x = 2, x = 3$

Lesson 13: Quadratic Equations

How to Answer

Step 1 Carefully read the question and decide what it is asking. You are being asked to find the *x*-intercepts of the given quadratic equation.

Step 2 You might plug values into the equation and plot the parabola on a coordinate grid.

Step 3 A good way to find the *x*-intercepts of a quadratic equation is to factor the equation. In this question $x^2 - 5x + 6 = 0$ is the original equation. You need to find two integers whose product is 6. That can be 6 and 1 or 2 and 3. Because the second term is $-5x$ and the last term is positive 6, you are going to want two negative integers. That would mean that you would use -2 and -3 because when they're added together, they equal -5 and when they're multiplied together, they equal $+6$. So the factor of the equation is $(x - 2)(x - 3) = 0$. Now solve each for *x*: $x - 2 = 0$ or $x = 2$ and $x - 3 = 0$ or $x = 3$. The *x*-intercepts are 2 and 3.

Step 4 Check your answer. Plug each of the values for *x* into the original equation and they should equal 0. $y = x^2 - 5x + 6$ or $y = 2^2 - 5(2) + 6$ or $y = 4 - 10 + 6$ or $y = 0$. When $x = 2$, the *y*-intercept is 0. So far, that looks good. Try the other value. $y = 3^2 - 5(3) + 6$ or $y = 9 - 15 + 6$ or $y = 0$. When $x = 3$, the *y*-intercept is 0. Good!

Step 5 Read all of the answer choices. Answer choices **A** and 2 have the wrong factors. Draw a line through them. Answer choice **C** has both values as negative numbers. That's not right. Draw a line through it. The only answer choice that has both 2 and 3 as positive numbers is **D**. If you did not get an answer that matched an answer choice, you can plug the values in the answer choices back into the original equation to see which pair of values fit. The one that fits is the right choice.

Step 6 You determined that answer choice **D** is correct. On the actual OGT you would fill in the appropriate bubble on your answer document, making sure that you are filling in the space for the correct question number and the correct answer choice.

Tip!

When you are factoring a quadratic equation, be especially careful to write the positive and negative signs clearly to avoid making a mistake later.

Now You Try It!

1. The fine for speeding on a highway is calculated with the equation

   $$F = x^2 - 5x$$

   where F is the amount of the fine and x is the number of miles per hour (mph) over the speed limit.

   If Mr. Stanley was caught driving 85 mph in a 65 mph speed limit zone, what fine would he have to pay?

   A. $220
   B. $260
   C. $300
   D. $395

2. What are the x-intercepts of the graph of the equation $y = x^2 - 2x - 24$?

   A. $x = 4, x = 6$
   B. $x = -4, x = 6$
   C. $x = 4, x = -6$
   D. $x = -4, x = -6$

Lesson 13: Quadratic Equations

3. Which equation would produce the results shown in the table below?

x	y
−1	4
0	0
1	−2
2	−2

A. $y = x^2 − 2x$
B. $y = x^2 − 3x$
C. $y = 2x^2 − x$
D. $y = 2x^2 − 2x$

4. Which expression is equivalent to $3x^2 − (2x + 5)x + (4x + 3)(x − 5)$?
A. $5x^2 − 28x − 15$
B. $4x^2 − 12x − 8$
C. $5x^2 − 22x − 15$
D. $9x^2 + 12x − 8$

5. Which expression below is equivalent to $2(6x + 4)^2$?

   A. $12x + 8$
   B. $36x^2 + 48x + 16$
   C. $72x^2 + 96x + 32$
   D. $144x^2 + 192x + 64$

6. Which equation would result in the parabola shown below?

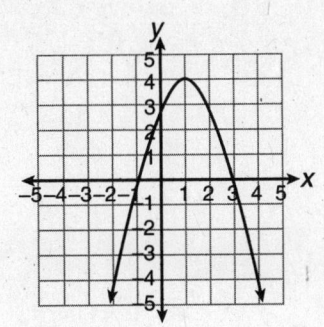

   A. $y = -x^2 + 2x + 3$
   B. $y = -x^2 - 2x + 3$
   C. $y = x^2 + 2x + 3$
   D. $y = x^2 - 2x + 3$

Lesson 13: Quadratic Equations

7. What are the x-intercepts of the graph of the equation $y = x^2 - 6x + 8$?

   A. $x = -2, x = -4$
   B. $x = -2, x = 4$
   C. $x = 2, x = -4$
   D. $x = 2, x = 4$

8. Which equation would produce the results shown in the table below?

x	y
0	0
1	2
2	8
3	18

   A. $y = x^2$
   B. $y = x^2 + 1$
   C. $y = x^2 + 2$
   D. $y = 2x^2$

LESSON 14
SYSTEMS OF EQUATIONS

> PATTERNS, FUNCTIONS, AND ALGEBRA H

About This Benchmark

The OGT will provide you with a system of equations, each equation with two variables. You will be asked to solve the equations algebraically. Some questions on the OGT may ask you to write two sets of equations to solve a problem.

VOCABULARY REVIEW

An **equation** is a mathematical statement that uses an equal sign (=). The values on either side of the equal sign are equal to each other.

Multiple-Choice Sample

▶ What is the solution to the following system of equations?

$$y = 3x + 1$$
$$x = y - 3$$

A. $x = -1, y = 2$
B. $x = 1, y = 4$
C. $x = 2, y = 5$
D. $x = 2, y = 7$

Lesson 14: Systems of Equations

Step 1 Carefully read the question and understand what it is asking. You need to determine which solution for x and y makes *both* equations true.

Step 2 You could work backward and plug in the values given in the answer choices. But some questions that test this skill will not provide you with answer choices, so try to solve this problem by using substitution.

Step 3 The system of equations given in the question stem each contain two variables, x and y. You can solve them together by using substitution. In the second equation $x = y - 3$. You can substitute $y - 3$ in place of x in the first equation. Then, you would have

$$y = 3x + 1$$
$$y = 3(y - 3) + 1$$
$$y = 3y - 9 + 1$$
$$y = 3y - 8$$
$$0 = 2y - 8$$
$$8 = 2y$$
$$4 = y$$

Now you have found the value of y so you can go back to either of the original equations and substitute 4 for y to find the value of x.

$$x = y - 3$$
$$x = 4 - 3$$
$$x = 1$$

Step 4 Check your answer by substituting the values of x and y into the other equation. Remember, the values have to work in *both* equations. $y = 3x + 1$ or $4 = 3(1) + 1$ or $4 = 4$.

Step 5 Read all of the answer choices. You can cross out answer choices **A, C,** and **D** because not even one of the values is correct. Only answer choice **B** has the correct values.

Step 6 On the actual OGT, you would now fill in the appropriate bubble on your answer document, making sure that you are filling in the space next to the correct question number and answer choice **B**.

Short-Answer Sample

▶ Anthony started his summer vacation with $100 in his savings account. He decided to deposit $80 per week into his account from his summer job. His sister Gail started her summer vacation with $600 in her savings account. She decided not to work and withdrew $20 per week.

Write two equations, one of the amount of money in Anthony's account x weeks after summer vacation started, and one for the amount of money in Gail's account x weeks after summer vacation started.

Determine the number of weeks until Anthony has more money in his account than Gail. Show your work or provide an explanation for your answer.

How to Answer

Step 1 Read the question carefully. You are to set up two equations and to determine when Anthony's account will have more money in it than Gail's account.

Step 2 You can set up the equations and then put them into an inequality to solve.

Step 3 Set up each equation first. Anthony has $100 and is going to put $80 per week, or $80x$, into his account. His equation would be $A = 100 + 80x$. Gail has $600 in her account, and she's going to withdraw $20 per week, or $-20x$. Her equation is $G = 600 - 20x$.

To find out how long it will take for Anthony to have more money in his account than Gail does in hers, set up an inequality: $100 + 80x > 600 - 20x$ and solve. $100x > 500$, or $x > 5$. This means that it will take Anthony 6 weeks to have more money in his account.

Lesson 14: Systems of Equations

Step 4 Check your answer. Another way to do find the same information and to check your answer is to set up a table.

Week	Anthony	Gail
1	180	580
2	260	560
3	340	540
4	420	520
5	500	500

In week 5, they have the same amount in their accounts. In week 6, Anthony will have more money in his account than in Gail's account.

Step 5 On the actual OGT, you would write each equation into your answer document, carefully labeling which is Anthony and which is Gail. Then, you would need to write a statement about when Anthony will have more money in his account. Your statement could look like the last line of Step 4.

Tip!

When given a system of equations, remember that it is impossible to solve either equation by itself. You need to solve one for either variable and plug that value into the other equation. Or, if you're given answer choices, you can plug those answers into both equations and see which answer choice works.

Now You Try It!

1. Solve the system of equations shown below.

$$3x - 8y = 16$$
$$x - y = 2$$

A. $x = 0, y = -2$
B. $x = 0, y = 2$
C. $x = 4, y = -2$
D. $x = 4, y = 2$

2. Train A left a station, picking up speed as it traveled along. When it was going 10 miles per hour, it began to pick up speed at a rate of 3 miles per hour for every mile it traveled. Train B was traveling at a speed of 80 miles per hour and slowed down at a rate of 11 miles per hour for every mile it traveled.

Write an equations for the rate of travel for Train A after it traveled m miles, and writer another equation for the rate of travel for Train B after it travel m miles.

Determine the number of miles until Train A and Train B will be going at the same rate of speed. Show your work or provide an explanation for your answer.

3. What is the solution to the system of equation below?

$$2y + 8 = 3x$$
$$x + 3y = 21$$

A. $x = 3, y = 5$
B. $x = 5, y = 6$
C. $x = 6, y = 5$
D. $x = 6, y = 6$

Lesson 14: Systems of Equations

4. Megan and her brother Sean collected stamps. Megan's collection had 30 stamps and she added 9 a month. Sean's collection had 17 stamps and he added 12 per month.

Write two equations—one for the number of stamps in Megan's collection after m months, and one for the number of stamps in Sean's collection after m months.

Determine the number of months until Sean has more stamps in his collection than Megan has in hers. Show your work or provide an explanation for your answer.

5. A system of equations is given below.

$$2x + 4y = 10$$
$$2y = 6x + 12$$

What is the solution for this system of equations?

A. $x = -1, y = -3$
B. $x = -1, y = 3$
C. $x = 1, y = -3$
D. $x = 1, y = 3$

LESSON 15
REPRESENTING DATA

> DATA ANALYSIS AND PROBABILITY A, B, AND F

About This Benchmark

You will be asked to interpret data that is displayed on graphs. You will also have to decide which type of graph is best to display certain kinds of data.

VOCABULARY REVIEW

A **box-and-whisker plot** is a specific way to display data that clearly indicates the minimum, maximum, median, and lower and upper quartiles of the data.

A **histogram** is a bar graph that contains no spaces between the bars. It is used to show the frequency with which data occurred. For example, if you surveyed your classmates to find out when their birthdays are, you could create a histogram that displayed the number of students who had birthdays in each month.

A **scatterplot** is a way to display data such that each individual point is plotted. For example, if you found out the height and weight of every student in your class, you could create a scatterplot that had height on the *y*-axis and weight on the *x*-axis. If someone was 5'3" and weighted 140 pounds, they would get an individual point at the point (140, 5'3").

Sample

▶ The table shows Jenna's marathon training schedule.

Jenna's Training

Week	Miles
1	14.3
2	16.5
3	17.2
4	25.3
5	28.6
6	30.2

Which type of graph would be the most appropriate to display the information from this table?

A. box-and-whisker plot
B. histogram
C. line graph
D. bar graph

How to Answer

Step 1 Read the question carefully. You are asked to look at the data and decide which type of graph would best display the data.

Step 2 You might try making some graphs to see which one best displays the data.

Step 3 Use POE to find the correct answer. Answer choice **A** is a box-and-whisker plot. This type of graph is used to divide a set of data into four different parts, using the quartiles and median. Jenna's table doesn't consist of this type of data so eliminate this answer choice. Answer choice **B** is a histogram, which organizes data into equal intervals and shows the frequency that the data occurred. That's not the type of graph you need for the data in the table. Eliminate this choice. Answer choice **C** is a line graph. A line graph best displays data that shows trends or changes over a period of time. If you used a line graph to show this information, you would see a line that goes up steadily as Jenna runs more miles per week. This seems right, but check answer choice **D** to be sure.

Answer choice **D** is a bar graph. A bar graph, like a histogram, organizes data into equal intervals and shows the frequency that the data occurred. Jenna could use this type of graph, but it would be less appropriate than the line graph.

Step 4 Using POE, you have determined that a line graph is the best way to display the data in the table. To check your answer, you might want to actually place the data into a line graph to make sure that displays the data well.

Step 5 On the actual OGT you would fill in the bubble on the answer document for answer choice **C**, making sure that you are filling in the correct number question.

Tip!

Some of the questions on the OGT may ask you to interpret data contained on a line graph, a scatterplot, or a box-and-whisker plot. Make sure that you know how to read each of these types of graphs.

Now You Try It!

1. The following box-and-whisker plot shows the heights of students in a science class.

   Heights of Students (inches)

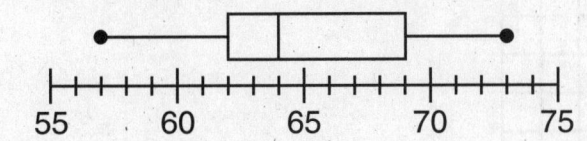

   55   60   65   70   75

   What statement can be made about the data, using the graph alone?

   A. The interquartile range is 9 inches.
   B. Fifty percent of the heights are above 65 inches.
   C. The median is 63 inches.
   D. The range is 16 inches.

Lesson 15: Representing Data

2. The graph below shows the population of the world from 1750 to 2000.

World Population (1750–2000)

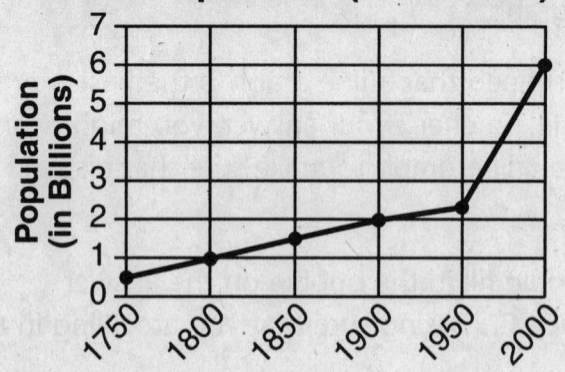

Based on the data, in which period did the world population increase the most?

A. 1800–1850

B. 1850–1900

C. 1900–1950

D. 1950–2000

3. The graph shows the amount of carbon dioxide (CO_2) emissions in the air between the years 1990 and 1999.

Carbon Dioxide Emissions

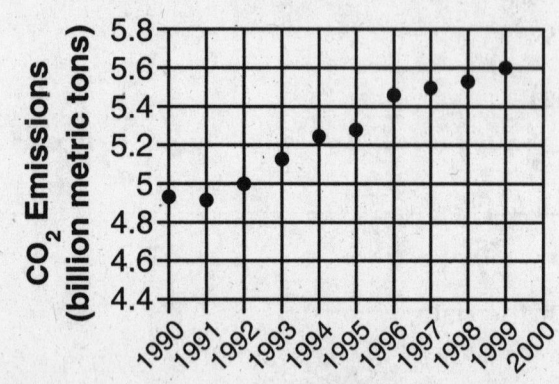

Based on the data, in which year did the emissions increase the most?

A. 1990–1991

B. 1993–1994

C. 1995–1996

D. 1998–1999

4. The following data consists of the weights, in pounds, of 40 adults.

   3 weighed   100–120
   6 weighed   121–140
   11 weighed 141–160
   12 weighed 161–180
   8 weighed   181–200

   Which of the following graphs is most appropriate to display this data?

   A. box-and-whisker plot
   B. histogram
   C. line graph
   D. scatterplot

5. The scatterplot shows the amount of time students spent on researching and writing a book report, and the grade they received for the book report.

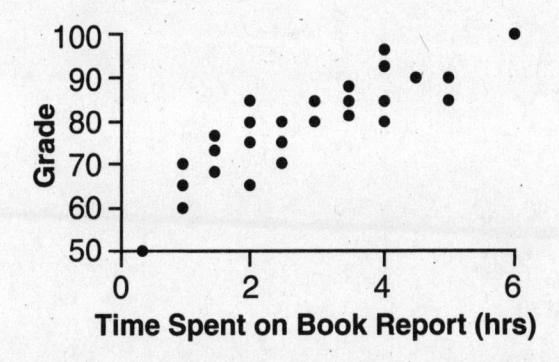

   What conclusion can be inferred from the data?

   A. The more time spent on the book report, the higher the grade.
   B. The time spent on the book report doesn't affect the grade.
   C. The less time spent on the book report, the higher the grade.
   D. The time spent on the book report and the grade are unrelated.

Lesson 15: Representing Data

6. Wendy recorded the low temperature in Akron, Ohio, over the course of the month of February. She wanted to put the data into a graph, so that she could see how much the low temperature fluctuated during the month.

   Which type of graph is appropriate to display Wendy's temperature data?

   A. box-and-whisker plot
   B. histogram
   C. line graph
   D. circle graph

7. The graph shows the relationship between the age of a painting and its value at auction.

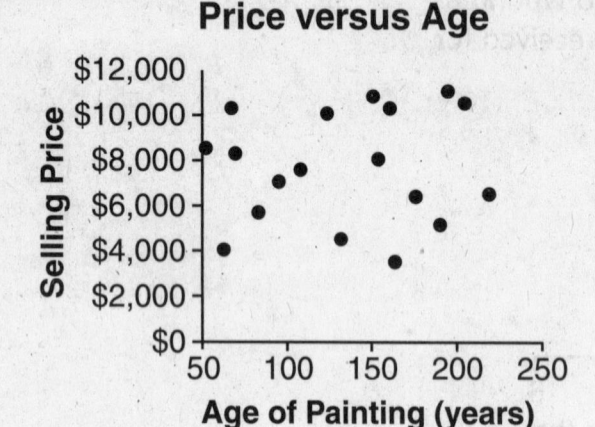

   Price versus Age

   What can be deduced from the data in the graph?

   A. As a painting gets older, its selling price increases.
   B. As a painting gets older, its selling price decreases.
   C. As a painting gets older, its selling price remains the same.
   D. The age of a painting and its selling price are not related.

LESSON 16
DATA SAMPLES AND MEAN, MEDIAN, AND MODE

> DATA ANALYSIS AND PROBABILITY C, D, E, AND G

About This Benchmark

You will need to be able to identify the mean, median, and mode of a set of data. Some questions on the OGT may ask you to determine how the sample of a survey should be chosen or if the information gained from a survey is valid.

VOCABULARY REVIEW

The **mean** is the average of the numbers in a set of data. The mean is calculated by adding the numbers in a set of data and then dividing that sum by the number of items of data.

The **median** is the middle number in a set of data when the data is ordered from least to greatest. If there is an even number of items of data in a set, the median is the mean of the 2 middle numbers.

The **mode** is the number(s) or item(s) that occurs the most often in a set of data. A set of data can have one mode, more than one mode, or it can have no mode.

A **representative sample** is a set of data that is expected to adequately reflect the population from which it was drawn.

If data is placed in order and divided into four equal groups, each group is called a **quartile.** The top 25% of the data represents the first quartile. The bottom 25% of the data represents the fourth quartile.

An **outlier** in a set of numerical data is a value that is significantly larger or smaller than the other values. It is the extreme number in a set. For example, the data set {8, 8, 7, 9, 7, 8, 44, 6, 8} would be 44.

Multiple-Choice Sample

▶ The mean of the daily high temperatures (Fahrenheit) in Cincinnati for five days was 51°. The temperatures over the first four days were 62, 59, 46, and 49. What was the temperature on the fifth day?

   A. 39°

   B. 41°

   C. 44°

   D. 54°

How to Answer

Step 1 — Carefully read the question and decide what it's asking. The question wants you to find the missing temperature that will give you a mean of 51°.

Step 2 — You could try working backward and guessing temperatures that might work. But you could also figure out the missing temperature by deducing what number must be added to the existing temperatures to equal 51° × 5.

Step 3 — You have to find the fifth temperature that will give a mean of 51° when included with the four other temperatures. Multiply 51 by 5 days to find what the total of the five days should be: 51 × 5 = 255. Now, add the temperatures from the four days: 62 + 59 + 46 + 49 = 216. Subtract 216 from 255 to find what the missing temperature is: 255 − 216 = 39. The missing temperature is 39°.

Step 4 — Check your answer. Add the five temperatures together and then find the mean: 62 + 59 + 46 + 49 + 39 = 255. Divide by 5: 255 ÷ 5 = 51°. That's right! By adding 39° to the four temperatures, you get a mean of 51°.

Step 5 — Read the answer choices. Answer choice **A** matches the answer you found. Review the others but none match the answer in Step 3 or Step 4. You can draw a line through them.

Step 6 — You determined that answer choice **A** is correct. On the actual OGT you would fill in the appropriate bubble on your answer document.

Short-Answer Sample

▶ A town wants to build a new, more modern building for the railroad station. The town council decides that a survey of the residents would be the best way to determine the amount of interest in the project. The three possible survey locations are the senior center, the grocery store, and the railroad station. Every third person at each location would be asked to participate in the survey.

Which of the proposed locations would provide the least bias in the survey? Explain your answer.

How to Answer

Step 1 Read the question carefully and make sure that you understand what it is asking. You may have underlined the words *least bias*.

Step 2 You might want to think about locations that would be biased to eliminate those answers.

Step 3 A survey location that would have the least bias is one that wouldn't involve people who have a direct interest in the proposed building. Anyone waiting at the railroad station for a train would be likely to want a more modern building. That survey location is not unbiased.

The senior center may not offer an unbiased survey because it would give the opinions of people who have the same interests. This site doesn't offer enough of a random sampling.

The grocery store would be the most unbiased location because the survey would result in the most random sampling of people with different interests.

Step 4 Check your answer by going through the choices again and making sure that you have a solid reason for your answer.

Step 5 Write your answer clearly. State why you chose your answer, as well as why you eliminated the other choices. Your statement might be: The grocery store would be the location with the least bias because all types of people would go there. The senior center would be biased because the people are older and might not take the train. The railroad station would be biased because the people there would likely want a building.

Tip!

Make sure you remember the meanings of mean, median, and mode. Find way to remember the meanings of these words. Here are some examples.

- In alphabetical order, the term **mean** comes first among the other terms. Likewise, the term average starts with a and comes first in the alphabet among the other definitions.
- **Median** is the middle number; median sounds a lot like the word medium, which also means middle.
- The **mode** is the number that occurs the most often; mode and most both begin with "mo-."

Now You Try It!

1. One set of data contains the following numbers: 18, 16, 15, 18, and 13. Which one of these statements must be true of this set of data?

   A. mean = mode
   B. mean = median
   C. median = mode
   D. mean > median

2. Fitness Gym wants to add a new weight machine to their equipment room.

   Which sample population should the gym survey to best represent the people who might use the new machine?

   A. survey each person who comes into the gym
   B. randomly survey the staff of the gym
   C. survey people passing by the gym
   D. randomly survey every fifth person who signs in at the gym

3. A set of data contains the numbers 35, 37, 39, 42, 46, 47, 51, and 93. If the outlier, 93, is removed from the set, which of the following statements must be true?

   A. The mean increases.
   B. The median increases.
   C. The mean decreases.
   D. The mode decreases.

4. Eight lab groups in science class found the boiling point of water (in degrees Celsius) to be: 98, 100, 97, 99, 102, 98, 101, 98. Which one of these statements must be true?

   A. mean = median
   B. median = mode
   C. mean > median
   D. mean < mode

Lesson 16: Data Samples and Mean, Median, and Mode

5. The mean height of the six members of the school basketball team is 73 inches. If three new members were added to the team, with the heights of 75, 76, and 77 inches, what is the mean height of the new team?

   A. 73 inches
   B. 74 inches
   C. 75 inches
   D. 76 inches

6. A museum is conducting a survey to see if there is interest in a meteorological exhibit. The survey must represent a cross-section of people in the museum's town. There are four possible survey locations: the entrance to the museum, the high school science classes, the community center, and the country club. Every fourth person at the location would be asked to participate in the survey.

   Which of the four proposed survey locations includes the least amount of bias? Be sure to provide an explanation for your answer.

LESSON 17
PROBABILITY, PERMUTATIONS, AND COMBINATIONS

> DATA ANALYSIS AND PROBABILITY H, I, J, AND K

About This Benchmark

You will be expected to compute the probabilities and predict the outcomes of events. Some questions on the OGT may ask you to determine the probability of a compound event. Other questions may ask you to make predictions based on probabilities and information.

VOCABULARY REVIEW

Probability is the likelihood that an event will happen. Probability is given as a number from 0 to 1. A probability of 0 means that an event will definitely not happen. A probability of 1 means that an event will definitely happen.

A **compound event** is an event that is comprised of 2 or more simple events.

A **permutation** is an arrangement of a set of items in a specific order.

A **combination** is a set of items in no particular order.

Independent events are events in which the result of one event does not affect the results of the other event.

Multiple-Choice Sample

▶ Sally has the following change in her purse: three quarters, two dimes, one nickel, and two pennies.

What is the probability that, if she picks a coin without looking, she will not pick a penny?

A. 12.5%

B. 25%

C. 50%

D. 75%

How to Answer

Step 1 Read the question carefully to understand what it's asking. You are to find the probability of Sally **not** picking a penny out of her purse. Be careful: You are looking for the probability that Sally will pick any coin from the purse *except* for a penny.

Step 2 You could use the numbers given to calculate the probability of Sally picking a penny, then subtracting that value from 1 to get the probability of her **not** picking the penny. (You could also draw a tree diagram to help visualize.)

Step 3 You need to find all of the possible outcomes. There are eight coins in Sally's purse so there are eight possible outcomes. Now, calculate the probability that the event described will occur. You do this by dividing the number of ways an event can occur by the number of possible outcomes. Because there are two pennies in Sally's purse, you would divide 2 by 8. $\frac{2}{8} = \frac{1}{4}$ = 25%. There is a 25% chance that the event will occur. To find the probability of the event not occurring, you subtract 25% from 100%: 100 − 25 = 75. There's a 75% probability that Sally will not pick a penny.

Step 4 Check your answer. Make sure that you've done the math correctly. Does your answer seem reasonable?

Step 5 Read all of the answer choices. Answer choice **A** is 25%, which is the probability that the event will occur. The question wants you to find the probability that event will **not** occur so this isn't the answer you want. Draw a line through it. Answer choices **B** and **C** aren't right either. You can cross them off. Answer choice **D** is 75%, which matches the answer you found in Step 3.

Step 6 On the actual OGT you would fill in the appropriate bubble for answer choice **D**, making sure to fill in the bubble next to the right question number.

Short-Answer Sample

▶ A bag of colored candies for a probability experiment contained 8 yellow, 10 red, and 6 green candies. A student removed 1 yellow, 2 red, and 1 green candy from the bag.

Did the loss of candies change the probability of drawing a red candy from the bag? If the answer is yes, was that probability increased or decreased? Show the probability for each situation.

How to Answer

Step 1 Read the question carefully and make sure you know what it's asking. You are asked to find if there is a difference in probability when some candies are removed from a bag. But you also need to say what that difference was, if there was a difference.

Step 2 You could create a tree diagram of both situations. But that might be too much work. It could be easier to calculate the probability before and after the candies are removed.

Step 3 The question wants you to decide if the probability is increased or decreased once some candies are removed from the bag. To do that, you will need to find the probability of both situations.

The bag initially has $8 + 10 + 6 = 24$ candies. There are 10 red ones: $\frac{10}{24} = \frac{5}{12} = 0.416$, or 42%. After candies are removed, there are: $7 + 8 + 5 = 20$ candies. There are 8 red ones: $\frac{8}{20} = \frac{2}{5} = 0.40$, or 40%. After the loss of candies in the bag, the probability of choosing a red candy decreases, going from 42% to 40%.

Step 4 Check your answer. You may want to review your figures for the probabilities before and after the loss of the candies. Make sure that you've used the right numbers and simplified them correctly.

Step 5 On the actual OGT, you must write your answer clearly and show your calculations on your answer document. This question wants to see your calculations and a written statement to support your answer for you to receive full credit.

Lesson 17: Probability, Permutations, and Combinations

> **Tip!**

Probability problems will often ask for the chances of an event not happening. Read carefully to make sure that you know which fraction of the possible outcomes is required for the answer. The probabilities of all possible outcomes for a particular problem will always add up to 1 (or 100%). For example, the probability of a fair coin landing on heads is $\frac{1}{2}$ (or 50%). The probability of the coin landing not landing on heads is $\frac{1}{2}$ (or 50%). You can add the 2 probabilities to get 1 (or 100%). The probability is 1 (100%) that the coin will land on either heads or tails.

> **Now You Try It!**

1. The table below shows the possible outcomes for the sum of two number cubes, number 1–6.

   Sums of Two Number Cubes

	\multicolumn{6}{c}{2nd Cube}
1st Cube	1	2	3	4	5	6
1	2	3	4	5	6	7
2	3	4	5	6	7	8
3	4	5	6	7	8	9
4	5	6	7	8	9	10
5	6	7	8	9	10	11
6	7	8	9	10	11	12

   What is the probability that the sum of the two number cubes will equal 9?

   A. $\frac{1}{18}$

   B. $\frac{1}{9}$

   C. $\frac{5}{36}$

   D. $\frac{1}{6}$

2. A bookshelf contains six mysteries and three biographies. Two books are selected at random without replacement.

   Determine the probability that both books are mysteries. Show your work or provide an explanation for your answer.

3. There are 15 boys and 10 girls in a mathematics class. Two students are chosen at random to work on the blackboard.

   What is the probability that both students are girls?

   A. 12%

   B. 15%

   C. 18%

   D. 20%

Lesson 17: Probability, Permutations, and Combinations

4   Alan, Becky, Jerry, and Mariah are four students in the chess club. Two of these students will be selected to represent the school at a national convention.

Determine how many combinations of two students are available. Show your work or provide an explanation for your answer.

5. The table below shows the number of United States flags sold each week for two months at a local store.

Number of Flags Sold Each Week

Week	1	2	3	4	5	6	7	8
Number of Flags Sold	3	4	6	1	5	0	2	1

If one of the weeks is chosen at random, what is the probability that at least 3 flags were sold that week?

A. $\frac{1}{4}$

B. $\frac{3}{8}$

C. $\frac{1}{2}$

D. $\frac{5}{8}$

Answer Key for Lessons

ANSWER KEY FOR LESSONS

Lesson 1: Numbers and Operations

1. The plumber's bill is $210 less the cost of parts of $48.50. 210 − 48.50 = $161.50. The plumber charges $38 per hour. 161.50 ÷ 38 = 4.25. The plumber worked 4.25 hours.

2. D

3. Thursday: 12,000 without power. Friday: 4,000 with power; 8,000 without power. Saturday: 1,000 lost power, making a total of 9,000 without power.

4. C

5. From tips, Bobbi takes home $200 − (20% × $200) = $200 − $40 = $160. From wages, she takes home $50 − (30% × $50) = $50 − $15 = $35. Her total take home after taxes is $160 + $35 = $195.

6. B
7. A

Lesson 2: Scientific Notation and Exponents

1. D
2. B
3. A
4. D
5. C
6. A
7. C
8. C
9. B
10. B
11. C
12. D
13. A
14. C
15. C

Lesson 3: Ratio, Proportion, and Percent

1. A
2. B
3. A
4. B
5. A
6. B
7. D
8. C

Lesson 4: Perimeter, Circumference, Area, and Volume

1. C
2. B
3. C
4. C
5. The surface area of the top and sides of the box is 120 in^2 + 500 in^2 + 150 in^2 = 770 in^2.
6. D
7. D
8. B
9. The area of the square is 36 yd^2. The area of one circle (2 semicircles) is 28.26 yd^2. The area of the semicircle is 14.13 yd^2. 36 + 28.26 + 14.13 = 78.39 or approximately 78 yd^2.

Lesson 5: Right Triangle Trigonometry

1. C
2. A
3. C
4. B
5. B
6. D

Lesson 6: Similarity and Congruence

1. A
2. D
3. B
4. A
5. C
6. D
7. C

Lesson 7: Geometric Figures and Coordinate Grids

1. B
2. C
3. B
4. A
5. C
6. B
7. C
8. B
9. D

Lesson 8: Angles and Lines

1. C
2. C
3. B
4. B
5. A
6. D

Answer Key for Lessons

Lesson 9: Transformations

1. D
2. A
3. The correct vertices of K'L'M' are (1, 3), (3, –2), and (–2, –1). The correct vertices of K"L"M" are (–4, 6), (–3, 1), and (–8, 2). The movement to translate from KLM to K"L"M" is ten units to the left and two units down.

Lesson 10: Patterns and Sequences

1. D
2. C
3. B
4. D
5. C
6. A
7. A

Lesson 11: Functions and Equations

1. D
2. A
3. B
4. B
5. D
6. C
7. D
8. C
9. C
10. A

Lesson 12: Inequalities

1. A
2. A
3. C
4. C
5. B
6. A
7. D
8. B
9. C
10. A

Lesson 13: Quadratic Equations

1. C
2. B
3. B
4. C
5. C
6. A
7. D
8. D

Lesson 14: System of Equations

1. A
2. Train A = 10 + 3m. Train B = 80 − 11m. The trains will be going at the same rate of speed at mile 5.
3. C
4. M = 30 + 9m. S = 17 + 12m. Sean will have more stamps in his collection in month 5.
5. B

Answer Key for Lessons

Lesson 15: Representing Data
1. D
2. D
3. D
4. B
5. A
6. C
7. C

Lesson 16: Data Samples and Mean, Median, and Mode
1. B
2. D
3. C
4. C
5. B
6. The community center would provide the least amount of bias because there would be a random sampling of people with different interests. The other locations would be likely to offer opinions of people who share a common interest.

Lesson 17: Probability, Permutations, and Combinations
1. B
2. The probability that the first book is a mystery is $\frac{6}{9}$; the probability that the second book is also a mystery is $\frac{5}{8}$. The probability of these two events happening back to back is $\frac{6}{9} \times \frac{5}{8} = \frac{30}{72}$.
3. B
4. $_4C_2 = \frac{4!}{(4-2)!2!} = \frac{12}{2} = 6$
5. C

Practice Tests

INTRODUCTION TO THE PRACTICE TESTS

By this point, you've made it through the lessons that review all of the skills that may be tested on the Mathematics Ohio Graduation Test (OGT). Congratulations! Now it's time to try your hand at a practice Mathematics OGT.

Each practice test in this book includes 37 multiple-choice questions, 5 short-answer questions, and 2 extended-response questions, totaling 44 questions in all. This is similar to what you can expect to see on the actual OGT.

An **Answer Document** precedes each practice test. Tear or cut out the pages of the **Answer Document**, and answer the questions on the practice test by filling in the bubbles and writing on the graphing area on the sheet. Use a No. 2 pencil, and take each practice test just as if you were taking the actual test. That means you should sit at a desk and avoid interruptions. Turn off the television, stereo, and even the telephone.

You will have up to two and a half hours to take the OGT for Mathematics. So when you take the practice test, you should set up a clock or alarm so you don't spend more than the allotted time. Plus, you should take the test in one sitting because you the administration of the actual Mathematics OGT will not be broken up into separate sittings.

Be sure to use the mathematics charts that precede each practice test. Tear or cut it out so you can use it while taking the practice tests. You'll be allowed to have a formula sheet similar to this one on the actual OGT. The sheet contains important information, such as conversion numbers and geometric formulas.

You can also use a graphing calculator on the OGT, so be sure you use one on the practice OGT as well. You should be as familiar as possible with the structure of the actual exam, so start with having a calculator handy! You'll also be provided with a ruler, so bring one along for the practice test too.

When you've completed the first practice test, check the answers and explanations for it on pages 233–246. Be sure to read through the explanations to all the questions—even the ones you got right. The explanations can help you figure out different ways to approach certain questions. The explanations for the second practice test are on pages 249–261.

When you're ready, cut out the mathematics chart and the **Answer Document** for the first practice test and get started. Good luck!

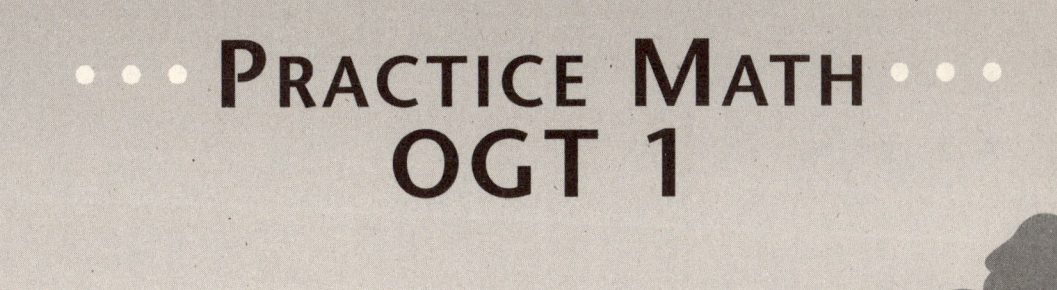

Practice Math
OGT 1

REFERENCE CHART FOR PRACTICE MATH OGT 1

Area Formulas

parallelogram $\quad A = bh$

rectangle $\quad A = lh$

trapezoid $\quad A = \frac{1}{2}h(b_1 + b_2)$

trapezoid $\quad A = \frac{1}{2}bh$

Volume Formulas

cone $\quad V = \frac{1}{2}\pi r^2 h$

cylinder $\quad V = \pi r^2 h$

pyramid $\quad V = \frac{1}{3}Bh \quad B = $ area of base

rectangular prism $\quad V = lwh$

right prism $\quad V = Bh \quad B = $ area of base

sphere $\quad V = \frac{4}{3}\pi r^3$

Circle Formulas

$C = 2\pi r \quad \pi \approx 3.14 \text{ or } \frac{22}{7}$

$A = 2\pi r^2$

Combinations

$_nC_r = C(n,r) = \frac{n!}{r(n-r)n!}$

Permutations

$_nP_r = P(n,r) = \frac{n!}{(n-r)!}$

Trigonometry

$\sin A = \frac{opposite}{hypotenuse}$

$\cos A = \frac{adjacent}{hypotenuse}$

$\tan A = \frac{opposite}{adjacent}$

Distance Formula

$d = \sqrt{(x_2 - x_1)^2 + (y_2 - y_1)^2}$

Quadratic Formula

$x = \frac{-b \pm \sqrt{b^2 - 4ac}}{2a}$

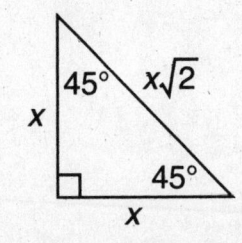

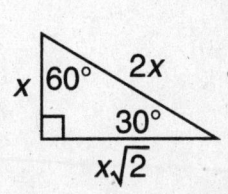

Practice Math OGT 1

ANSWER DOCUMENT FOR PRACTICE MATH OGT 1

1. Ⓐ Ⓑ Ⓒ Ⓓ
2. Ⓐ Ⓑ Ⓒ Ⓓ
3. Ⓐ Ⓑ Ⓒ Ⓓ
4. Ⓐ Ⓑ Ⓒ Ⓓ
5. Ⓐ Ⓑ Ⓒ Ⓓ
6. Ⓐ Ⓑ Ⓒ Ⓓ
7. Ⓐ Ⓑ Ⓒ Ⓓ
8. Two-point short-answer question:

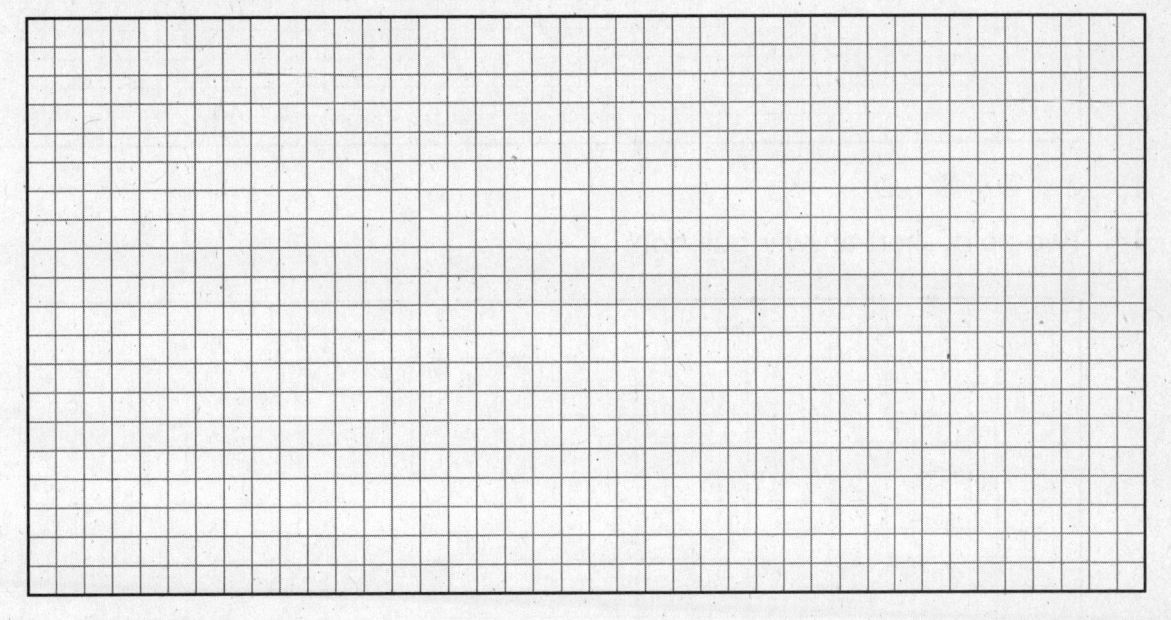

9. Ⓐ Ⓑ Ⓒ Ⓓ
10. Ⓐ Ⓑ Ⓒ Ⓓ
11. Ⓐ Ⓑ Ⓒ Ⓓ

Practice Math OGT 1

12. Two-point short-answer question:

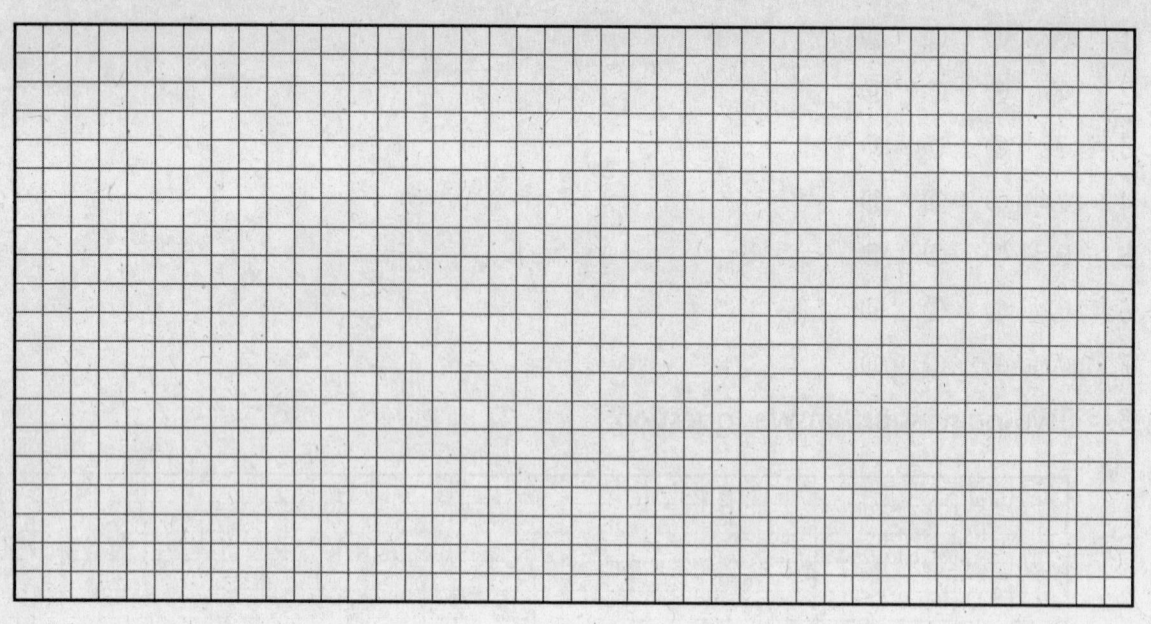

13. Ⓐ Ⓑ Ⓒ Ⓓ

14. Two-point short-answer question:

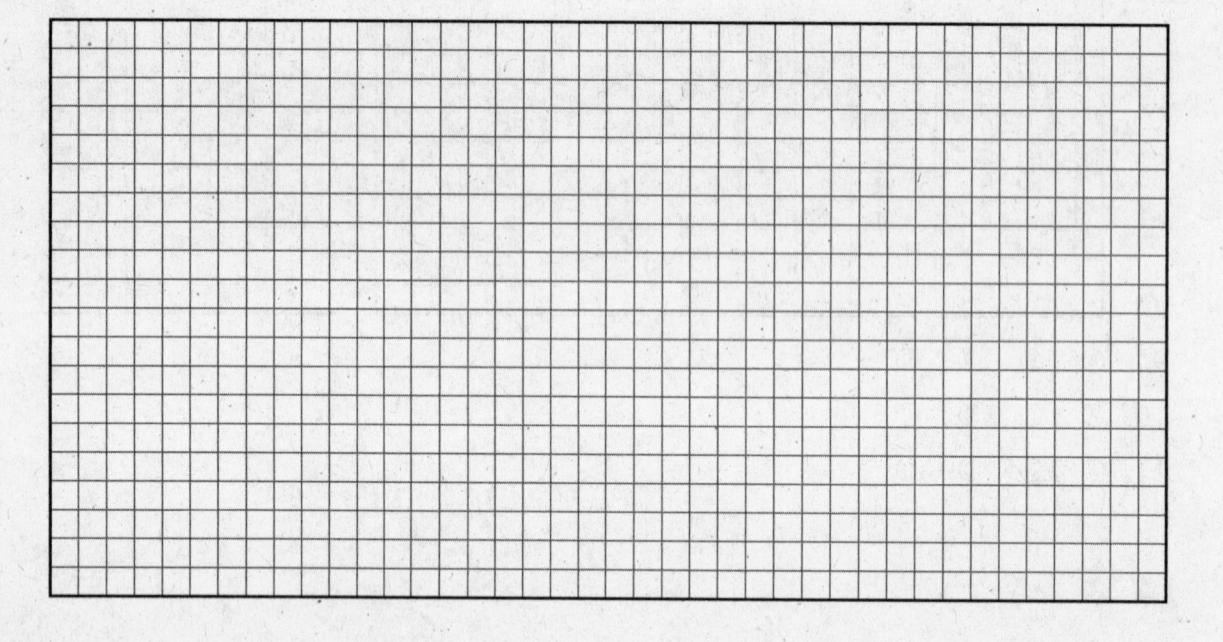

15. Ⓐ Ⓑ Ⓒ Ⓓ
16. Ⓐ Ⓑ Ⓒ Ⓓ
17. Ⓐ Ⓑ Ⓒ Ⓓ
18. Ⓐ Ⓑ Ⓒ Ⓓ
19. Four-point extended-response question:

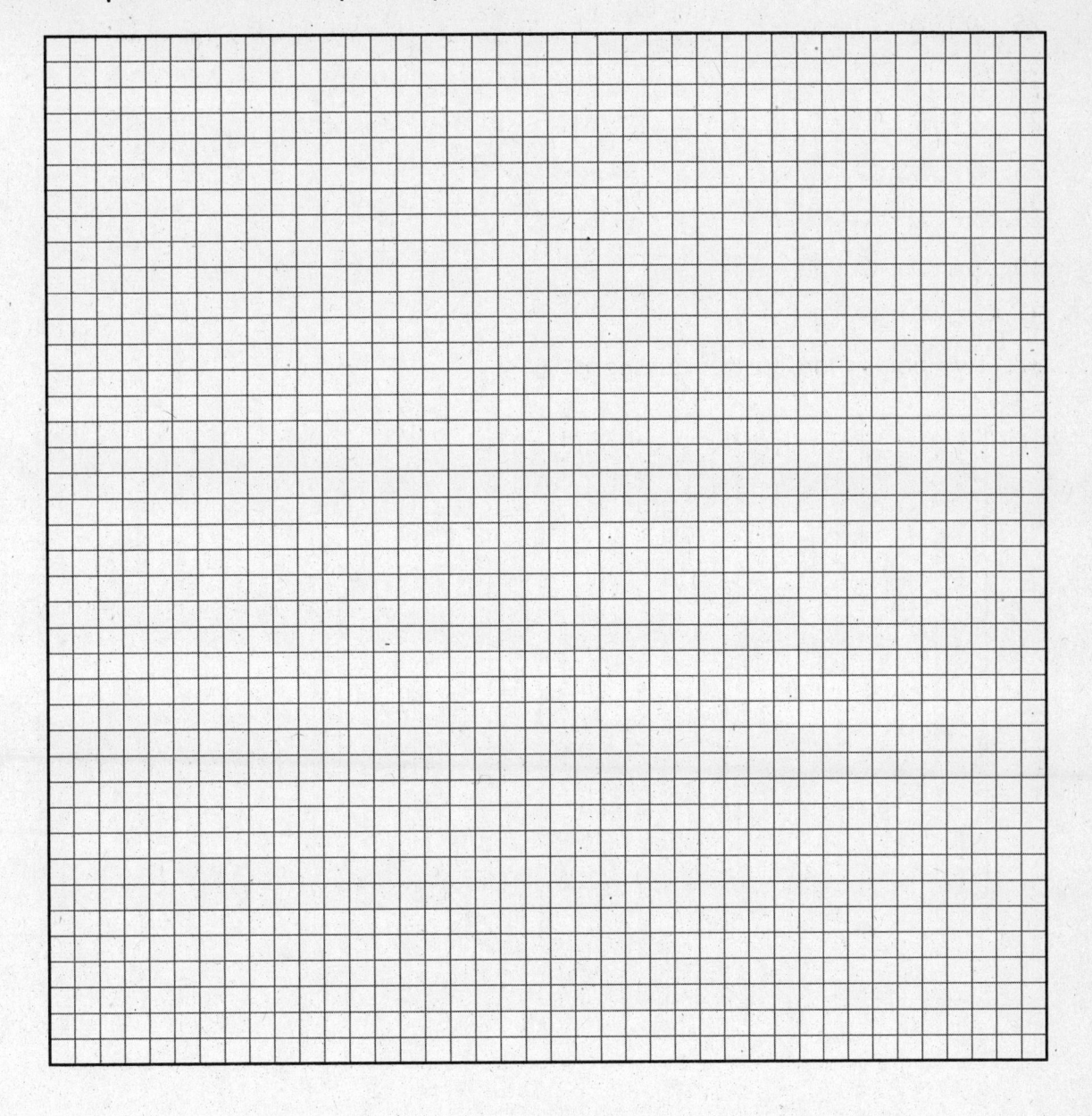

Practice Math OGT 1

20. Ⓐ Ⓑ Ⓒ Ⓓ
21. Ⓐ Ⓑ Ⓒ Ⓓ
22. Ⓐ Ⓑ Ⓒ Ⓓ
23. Ⓐ Ⓑ Ⓒ Ⓓ
24. Ⓐ Ⓑ Ⓒ Ⓓ
25. Ⓐ Ⓑ Ⓒ Ⓓ
26. Ⓐ Ⓑ Ⓒ Ⓓ
27. Ⓐ Ⓑ Ⓒ Ⓓ
28. Ⓐ Ⓑ Ⓒ Ⓓ
29. Ⓐ Ⓑ Ⓒ Ⓓ
30. Ⓐ Ⓑ Ⓒ Ⓓ
31. Ⓐ Ⓑ Ⓒ Ⓓ
32. Two-point short-answer question:

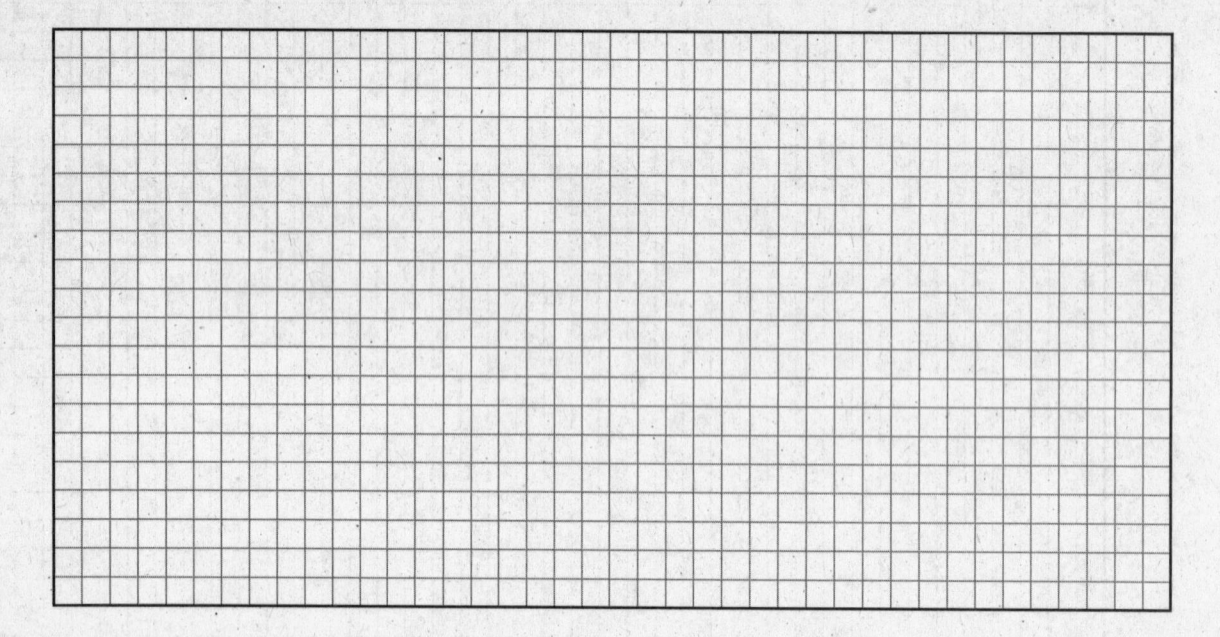

33. Ⓐ Ⓑ Ⓒ Ⓓ
34. Ⓐ Ⓑ Ⓒ Ⓓ
35. Ⓐ Ⓑ Ⓒ Ⓓ
36. Ⓐ Ⓑ Ⓒ Ⓓ
37. Ⓐ Ⓑ Ⓒ Ⓓ
38. Ⓐ Ⓑ Ⓒ Ⓓ
39. Ⓐ Ⓑ Ⓒ Ⓓ
40. Ⓐ Ⓑ Ⓒ Ⓓ
41. Two-point short-answer question:

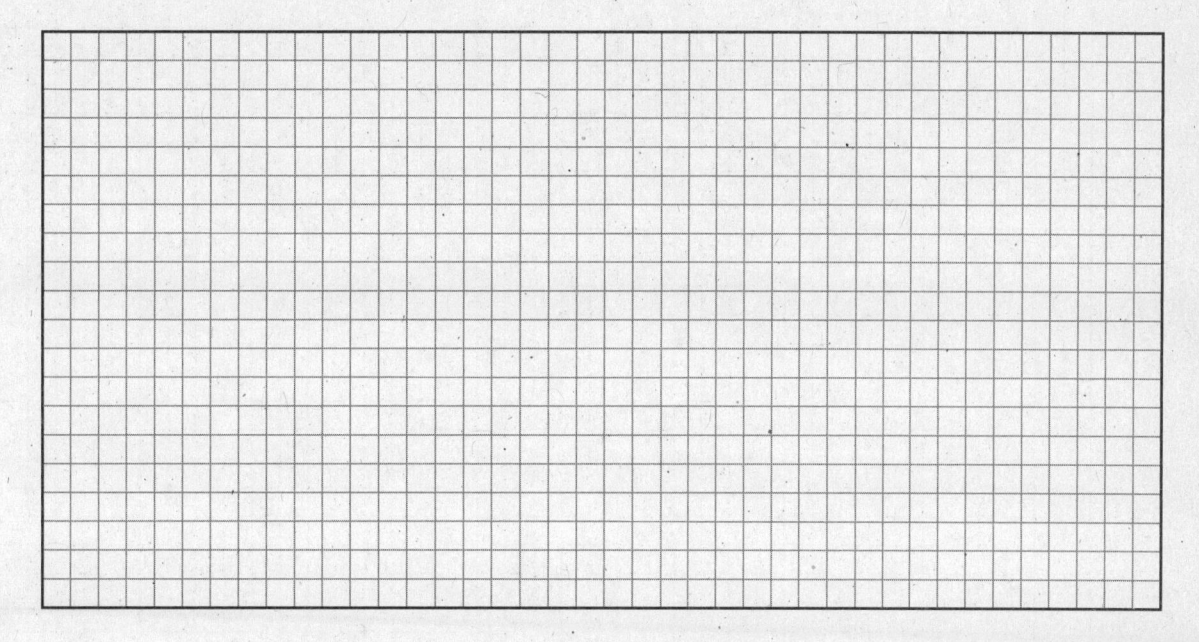

Practice Math OGT 1

42. Ⓐ Ⓑ Ⓒ Ⓓ
43. Four-point extended-response question:

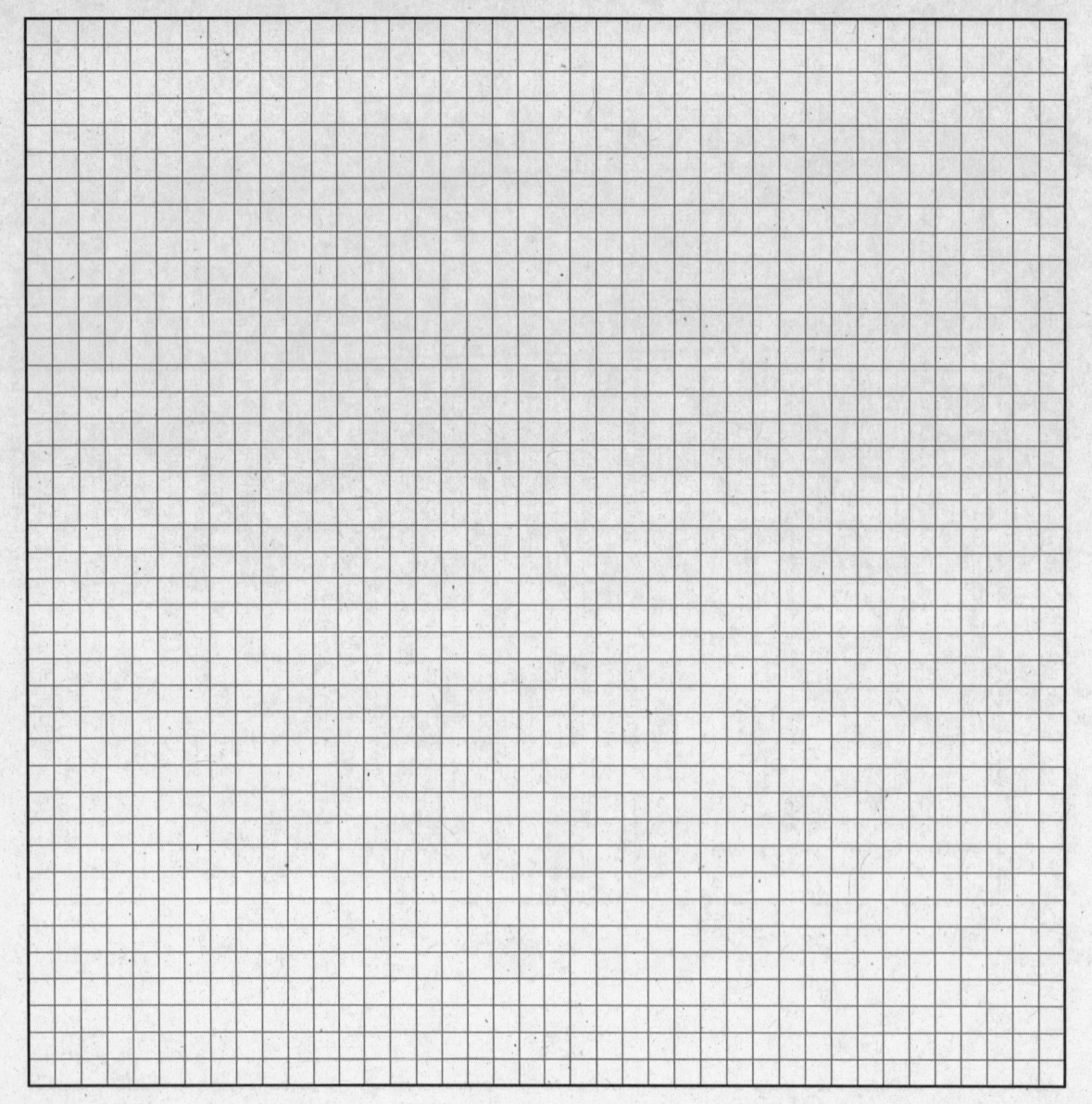

44. Ⓐ Ⓑ Ⓒ Ⓓ

PRACTICE MATH OGT 1

Directions: The practice math OGT contains 44 questions: 37 multiple-choice questions, 5 short-answer questions, and 2 extended-response questions. When answering the multiple-choice questions, solve each problem and then fill in the correct answer choice on the Answer Document. When answering the short-answer and extended-response questions, be sure that you answer completely and that all of your work is contained in the Answer Document. *Only the Answer Document will be scored.*

---

1. Charles plans to use each of the letters A, B, C, D, E, F, and G once to create a seven-letter password for his computer. He wants the letter A to be the second letter in the password but otherwise doesn't care about the order of the letters.

    How many different combinations of letters are available to Charles?

    A. 6
    B. 120
    C. 720
    D. 5,040

Go to next page

2. Peter has a swimming pool that is 6 meters wide, 12 meters long, and 2 meters deep. 1,000 liters of water fills 1 cubic meter.

   How many liters of water are required to fill Peter's pool to the top?

   A. 144 liters
   B. 64,000 liters
   C. 96,000 liters
   D. 144,000 liters

3. The pattern below shows the seating in an auditorium.

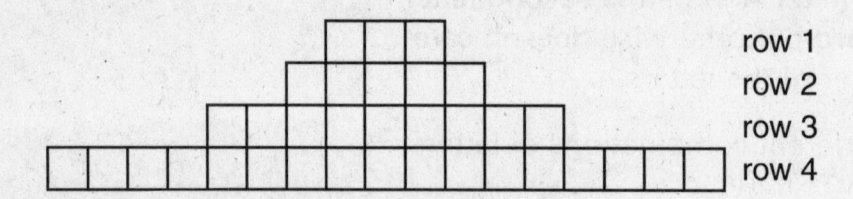

   If this pattern continues, how many squares would make up row 6 of the pattern?

   A. 33
   B. 65
   C. 67
   D. 122

Go to next page

4. The box-and-whisker plot shown below describes the results of a survey of students asking how many movies they rented from a video store last month.

Number of Movies Rented Last Month

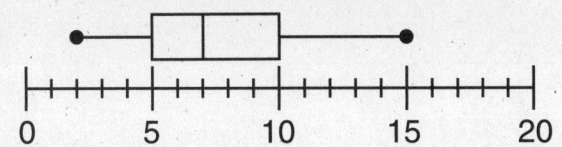

Which is a true statement in regards to the data from the graph?

A. Fifty percent of the students rented fewer than 5 movies last month.

B. The range of the number of movies rented last month was 10.

C. The median number of movies rented last month was 7.

D. Fifty percent of the students rented more than 10 movies last month.

5. Which of the following numbers is irrational?

A. $\sqrt{9}$

B. $\sqrt{8}$

C. $0.33\overline{3}$

D. $\frac{2}{3}$

Go to next page

Practice Math OGT 1

6. Points A and B are shown in the graph below.

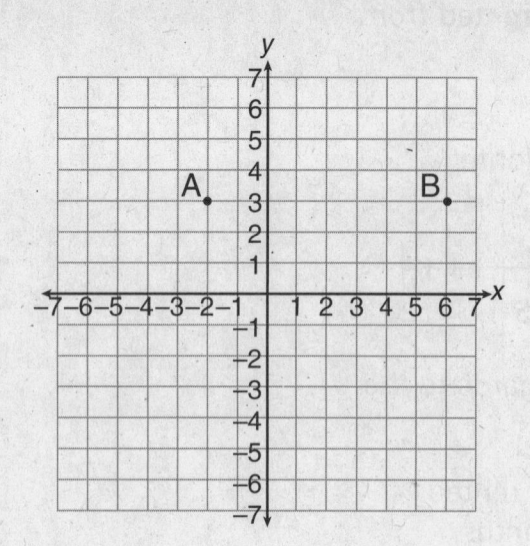

Points A and B are two vertices of a rectangle. What could be the coordinates of the other two vertices, C and D, to form rectangle ABCD?

A. (6, 6) and (−1, 6)
B. (3, 6) and (3, −2)
C. (−2, −6) and (3, 3)
D. (−2, −1) and (6, −1)

7. Leslie has taken 6 exams in her chemistry class. She received grades of 93, 88, 85, 92, 89, and 92 on those tests. Which one of the following must be true?

A. mean = 89.93
B. median = 85
C. mode = 92
D. range = 7

8. A circular carpet is placed in a square room and stretches from one side of the room to the other. The radius of the carpet is 6 feet.

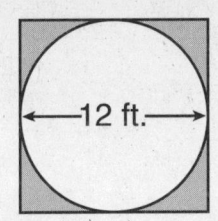

←—12 ft.—→

Find the area of the floor **not** covered by the carpet. Write your answer in square feet in your **Answer Document**. Be sure also to show all your work or explain how your answer was found.

For question number 8, use the separate **Answer Document** for your complete response. This question is worth 2 points.

Go to next page

Practice Math OGT 1

9. Kim and her friends had lunch at a restaurant. The bill was $65. The manager then gave them a $10 discount because they had to wait a long time for their food. The girls gave the waiter a tip on the final bill. They paid a total of $66.

   What percent did the girls leave as a tip?

   A. 0.08%
   B. 20%
   C. 25%
   D. 80%

10. Aleesha earned money during the summer by babysitting for her neighbor's children. During one a five-day period, she earned $26, $38, $20, $46, and $35. If she wanted to earn a mean of $35 a day, how much would she have to earn on the sixth day?

    A. $28
    B. $33
    C. $35
    D. $45

Go to next page

11. The line on the graph below represents a linear equation.

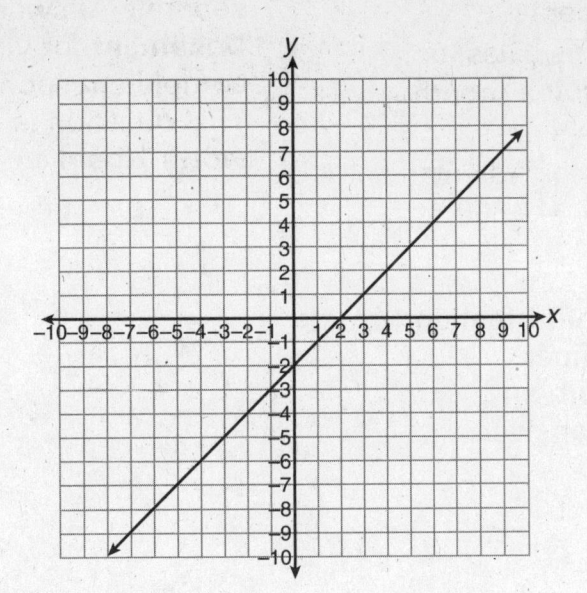

Which of the following equations represents the graphed line?

A. $y = x + 2$
B. $y = x - 2$
C. $y = x + 4$
D. $y = x - 4$

Go to next page

Practice Math OGT 1

12. Stephen is offered a job selling furniture. His employer gives him a choice of payment plans: he can either accept a straight commission of 20% on his sales, or he can take a base salary of $1,000 a month plus a commission of 10% on his sales. Stephen expects his sales to be equivalent to the last three months of sales: $12,500, $16,000, and $13,000.

    Which payment plan would benefit Stephen the most? Show your work and final answer in your **Answer Document**, and provide an explanation for your answer.

    *For question number 12, use the separate **Answer Document** for your complete response. This question is worth 2 points.*

13. The table below shows values for *x* and *y*.

x	y
−1	−10
0	−12
1	−12
2	−10

    Which of these equations represents the relationship between *x* and *y*?

    A. $y = x - 12$
    B. $y = x^2 + x - 10$
    C. $y = -2(x + 6)$
    D. $y = (x + 3)(x - 4)$

Go to next page

162   Roadmap to the Ohio Graduation Test: Mathematics

14. A 10th-grade social studies class wants to write an article on city and state government for the local newspaper each week. The class feels that they will have a better chance of convincing the editor of the paper to include their article if they have community support of adults. They hope to prove this support with a survey of random sampling. The class debates three survey sites are proposed: a supermarket, a senior citizens center, and outside the high school. Every fourth person at each location would be asked if they would be interested in reading an article written by a 10th grader.

    In your **Answer Document**, explain which, if any, of the three survey locations provide enough of a sampling of the community. Explain your answer.

For question number 14, use the separate **Answer Document** for your complete response. This question is worth 2 points.

15. Enzo gives Thomas 569 poems to make into a book. Thomas decides to print 394 of the poems.

    Which expression can be used to determine the percent of Enzo's poems that Thomas did **not** print?

    A. $\frac{394}{569} \times 100$

    B. $\frac{569}{394} \times 100$

    C. $\frac{(394-569)}{569} \times 100$

    D. $\frac{(569-394)}{569} \times 100$

Go to next page

Practice Math OGT 1

16. Mrs. Matsumoto decides to create a sandbox for her kids and fill it with sand that is sold by the bucket. Each bucket is cylindrical, with the dimensions shown below.

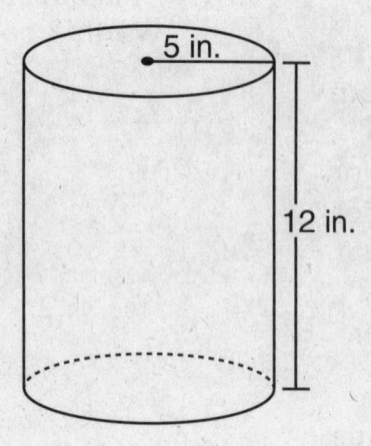

5 in.

12 in.

Approximately how many buckets of sand will Mrs. Matsumoto need to fill a sandbox that is 5 feet wide, 5 feet long, and 6 inches deep?

A. 23
B. 180
C. 360
D. 940

17. Kim kept track of the temperatures on her farm during the entire year. For the first two months of the year, the temperature was about the same. There was a gradual rise through June. The temperatures spiked during July and August and then gradually got cooler through to December. Which graph best shows this information?

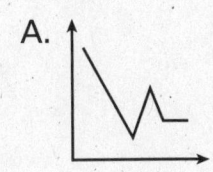

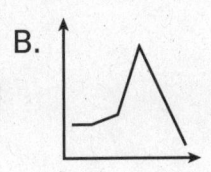

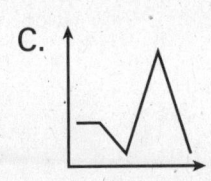

A.

B.

C.

D.

Go to next page

Practice Math OGT 1

18. The table below represents all the possible outcomes for the sum of two number cubes, numbered 1–6.

Sums of Two Number Cubes

	\multicolumn{6}{c}{2nd Cube}
1st Cube	1	2	3	4	5	6
1	2	3	4	5	6	7
2	3	4	5	6	7	8
3	4	5	6	7	8	9
4	5	6	7	8	9	10
5	6	7	8	9	10	11
6	7	8	9	10	11	12

What is the probability that the sum of the two number cubes will equal 7?

A. $\frac{1}{18}$

B. $\frac{1}{9}$

C. $\frac{1}{7}$

D. $\frac{1}{6}$

Go to next page

19. Triangle ABC has three vertices. The coordinates of those vertices are A(2, −6), B(4, −2), and C(6, −4).

    Draw and label the triangle ABC on the grid that you will find in your **Answer Document**.

    The triangle A'B'C' can be found by translating each vertex of ABC two units to the right and then six units up. Draw and label A'B'C' on the grid.

    The triangle A"B"C" can be found by translating each vertex of A'B'C' five units to the left and then three units down. Draw and label A"B"C" on the grid.

    What movements would you need to translate each vertex from triangle ABC to triangle A"B"C"?

For question number 19, use the separate **Answer Document** for your complete response. This question is worth 4 points.

20. Which of the following shows the correct order from *least* to *greatest*?

    A. $|-0.9|$, $\frac{4}{5}$, $\sqrt{0.49}$, 0.622

    B. $\frac{4}{5}$, 0.622, $|-0.9|$, $\sqrt{0.49}$

    C. 0.622, $\sqrt{0.49}$, $\frac{4}{5}$, $|-0.9|$

    D. $\sqrt{0.49}$, $|-0.9|$, $\frac{4}{5}$, 0.622

Go to next page

Practice Math OGT 1

167

21. Damian wants to move a 600-kilogram pile of sand from one end of his yard to the other. He decides to move 200 kilograms the first day. On each subsequent day, he will move one-quarter of the amount of sand he moved the previous day.

    How much sand will Damian have moved after 4 days?

    A. $265\frac{5}{8}$ kilograms

    B. $266\frac{3}{32}$ kilograms

    C. $337\frac{1}{2}$ kilograms

    D. 400 kilograms

22. The hourly temperatures in Beijing, China, over a 4-hour period on January 16 are 10:00 a.m. 32°, 11:00 a.m. 34°, 12:00 p.m. 40°, 1:00 p.m. 42°, and 2:00 p.m. 44°.

    Which type of graph is most appropriate to illustrate this data?

    A. bar graph
    B. box-and-whisker plot
    C. line graph
    D. scatterplot

Go to next page

23. David wants to cover the box below with self-adhesive paper. All 6 faces must be covered.

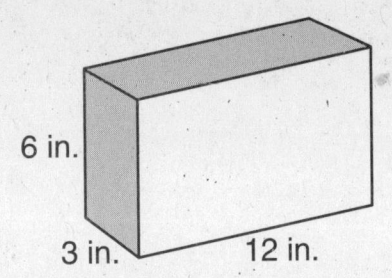

6 in.
3 in. 12 in.

What is the total surface area of all 6 faces of the box?

A. 108 square inches
B. 126 square inches
C. 216 square inches
D. 252 square inches

Go to next page

Practice Math OGT 1

169

24. Four coins, a penny (P), a nickel (N), a dime (D), and a quarter (Q) are placed in a bag. Without looking Hakeem picks one coin, replaces it, and then picks a coin again. The tree diagram shown below represents all the possible outcomes.

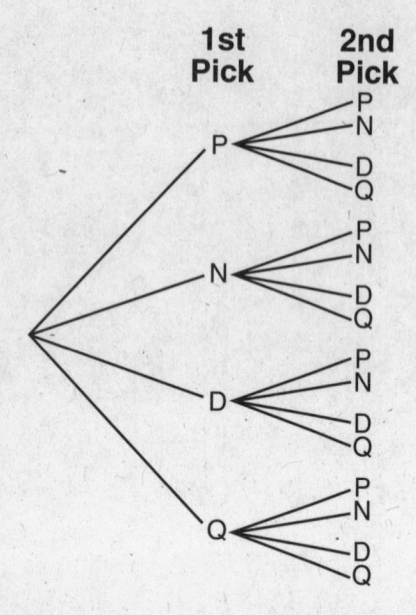

What is the probability that the total value of the coins Hakeem picks will be exactly $0.35?

A. $\frac{1}{16}$

B. $\frac{1}{8}$

C. $\frac{1}{4}$

D. $\frac{1}{2}$

Go to next page

25. Which figure is similar to triangle PQR?

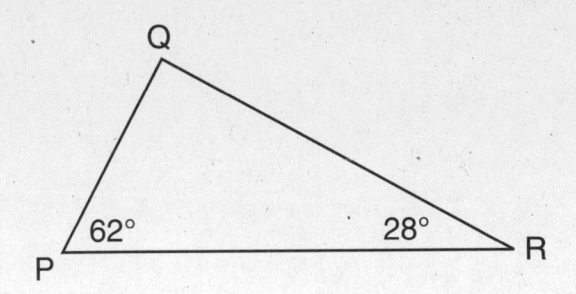

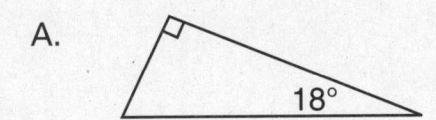

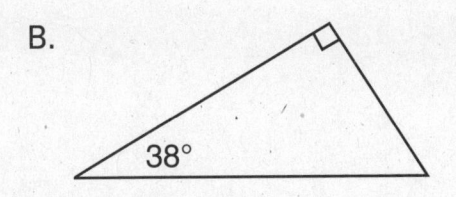

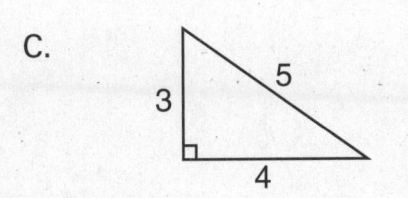

A. 18°

B. 38°

C. 3, 4, 5 right triangle

D. 62°

Go to next page

Practice Math OGT 1

26. How would the scientific notation 1.8×10^{-3} be written in standard form?

   A.   0.0018

   B.   0.018

   C.   180

   D.   1,800

27. The nurses at a hospital charted the weights of all babies born in the hospital that week. A few of the weights were very low. Which measure of central tendency best describes the typical birth weight of the babies born during the week?

   A. mean

   B. median

   C. mode

   D. range

Go to next page

28. Which of the following graphs represents the graph of the inequality $y < 4x - 3$?

A.

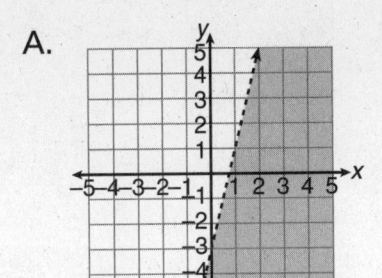

B.

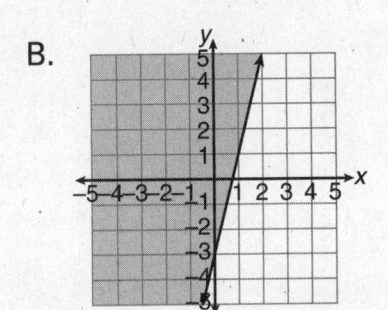

C.

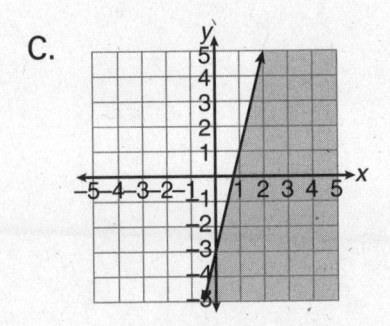

D.

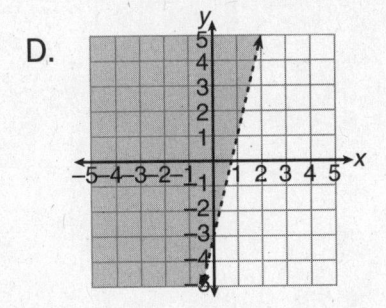

Go to next page

Practice Math OGT 1

29. Which of the following equations is equivalent to the equation
    $7(9 - 2y) = 5(y + 8)$?

    A. $23 = -19y$

    B. $23 = 19y$

    C. $103 = 9y$

    D. $103 = -9y$

30. Using her calculator, Seema found the volume of the cylinder shown below to be 389.7167 cm³. She knew she had made an error.

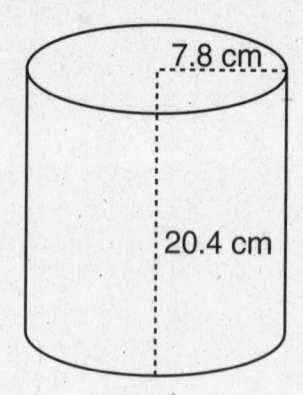

    7.8 cm

    20.4 cm

    What should be the approximate volume of the cylinder?

    A. 1,440 cm³

    B. 3,840 cm³

    C. 5,024 cm³

    D. 10,240 cm³

Go to next page

31. One of the triangles below shows the measure of its line segments. The other triangle gives the measure of two of its angles.

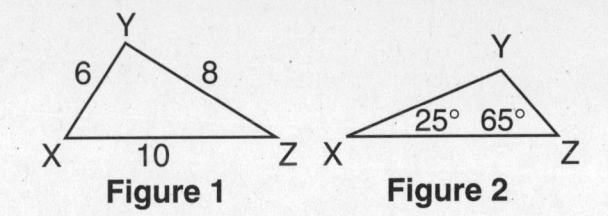

Figure 1: Triangle XYZ with XY = 6, YZ = 8, XZ = 10.

Figure 2: Triangle XYZ with angle X = 25°, angle Z = 65°.

What do you know is true about the two triangles?

A. They are right triangles.
B. They are isosceles triangles.
C. Their sides are congruent.
D. Their angles are congruent.

For question number 32, use the separate **Answer Document** for your complete response. This question is worth 2 points.

32. Katrina had $200 in her bank account at the beginning of the summer. She worked all summer and added $300 to her bank account each week during the summer. Evan had $2,650 in his account at the beginning of the summer, decided not to work, and spent $50 each week during the summer.

Write two equations in your **Answer Document**: one equation should be for the amount of money in Katrina's bank account x weeks after the summer starts, and the other equation should be for the amount of money in Evan's bank account x weeks after the summer starts.

Figure out how many weeks will pass until Katrina's bank account will have more money than Evan's bank account. Be sure to show your work or explain your answer in your **Answer Document**.

Go to next page

Practice Math OGT 1   175

33. Which 3-dimensional figure has the greatest number of 4-edged faces?

   A. rectangular prism

   B. rectangular pyramid

   C. triangular prism

   D. triangular pyramid

34. At a large department store, customers take an escalator to the second floor. The escalator has a 30° angle of inclination and rises 20 feet high.

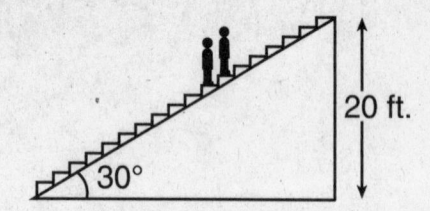

   What is the approximate diagonal distance the escalator travels between floors?

   A. 10 feet

   B. $20\sqrt{2}$ feet

   C. $20\sqrt{3}$ feet

   D. 40 feet

Go to next page

35. Simone can only spend $200 on party favors for the eleventh-grade homecoming dance. She had chosen picture frames, x, and Frisbees, y. Each frame costs $3.95 and each Frisbee costs $3.50.

   Which inequality should Simone use to determine the maximum number of each party favor she can buy without spending more than $200?

   A. $3.50x + 3.95y < 200$
   B. $3.95x + 3.50y \leq 200$
   C. $3.50x + 3.95y \leq 200$
   D. $3.95x + 3.50y \geq 200$

36. The staff of Good Reading bookstore wants to see how many books are read each month by people who participate in the reading groups that meet in the store.

   Which population should be surveyed to represent the average participant in the reading groups?

   A. randomly survey people entering the bookstore
   B. survey only the people who buy books
   C. randomly survey three members of each reading group
   D. survey people over 21

Go to next page

Practice Math OGT 1

37. On the map shown below, Sixth Avenue runs parallel to Seventh Avenue. Bob walks uptown on Sixth Avenue, turns left 30°, and walks to Seventh Avenue. When he reaches Seventh Avenue, he turns right onto Seventh Avenue.

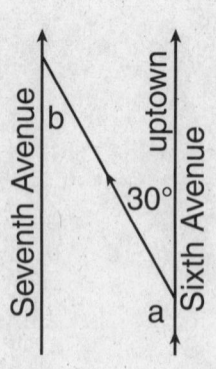

What are the measures of angles *a* and *b*, respectively?

A. 150°, 30°
B. 30°, 30°
C. 30°, 180°
D. 150°, 150°

38. A cardboard box has a length of 33 centimeters and a width of 24 centimeters. A smaller cardboard box with similar proportions fits inside the larger one. It has a width of 8 centimeters.

What is the length of the smaller cardboard box?

A. 5 centimeters
B. 6 centimeters
C. 9 centimeters
D. 11 centimeters

Go to next page

39. The graph below shows the amount of whole milk consumed per person in the United States from 1965 to 1995.

U.S. Whole Milk Consumption

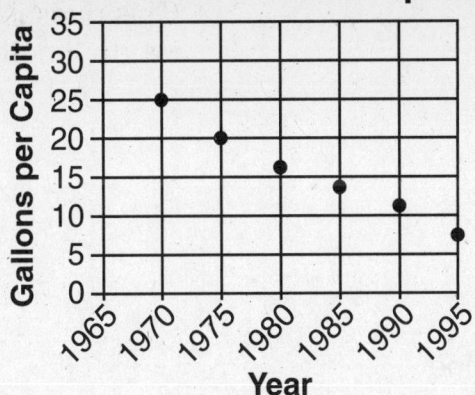

Based on the data, what is the most likely value for gallons of whole milk consumed per capita in 1965?

A. 20
B. 23
C. 25
D. 29

40. A system of equations is given below.

$$3x = 7y + 1$$
$$x = y - 1$$

Which of the following lists the solution to the system of equations?

A. $x = -5, y = -2$
B. $x = -2, y = -1$
C. $x = 2, y = 3$
D. $x = 5, y = 2$

Go to next page

Practice Math OGT 1

41. A clothing store holds a special sale during which customers may buy 5 shirts for $100.00 or they may take 15% off the ticketed price of each shirt. Oswald brought 5 shirts to the cash register. The ticketed prices of the shirts were

$25.75

$21.45

$18.05

$24.80

$29.80

In your **Answer Document**, determine which option is the better bargain for Oswald: 5 shirts for $100, or 15% off the ticketed price of the shirts. Be sure to show your work or provide an explanation for your answer in your **Answer Document**.

For question number 41, use the separate **Answer Document** for your complete response. This question is worth 2 points.

Go to next page

42. Tiba wanted to know the height of a tree in his yard. He placed a 72-inch pole next to the tree and measured the shadow it cast along the ground. The shadow was 120 inches long. Then, Tiba measured the shadow that the tree cast along the ground. The shadow of the tree was 420 inches.

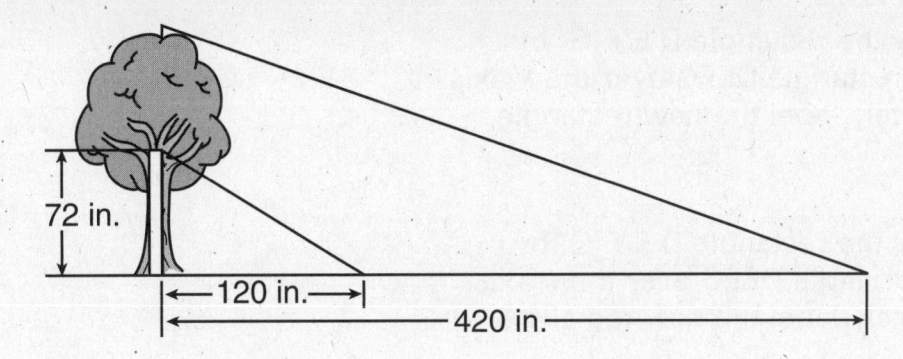

How tall is the tree?

A. 180 inches
B. 252 inches
C. 348 inches
D. 420 inches

Go to next page

Practice Math OGT 1

43. Rectangle DEFG has four vertices with the following coordinates:

   D(3, 4), E(7, 4), F(3, 1), and G(7, 1)

   Use the grid in your **Answer Document** to draw and label the rectangle DEFG.

   Then draw the rectangle D'E'F'G' by reflecting rectangle DEFG over the *x*-axis. Appropriately label the new rectangle D'E'F'G'.

   Then draw the rectangle D"E"F"G" by reflecting triangle DEFG over the *y*-axis. Appropriately label the new rectangle D"E"F"G".

   Describe the mathematical operation that is necessary to reflect the coordinates of a figure over the *x*-axis.

   Describe, in your **Answer Document**, the mathematical operation necessary to reflect the coordinates of a figure over the *x*-axis and the *y*-axis.

For question number 43, use the separate **Answer Document** for your complete response. This question is worth 4 points.

Go to next page

44. Which of the graphs shown below best represents the graph of the equation $y = 1 + x^2$?

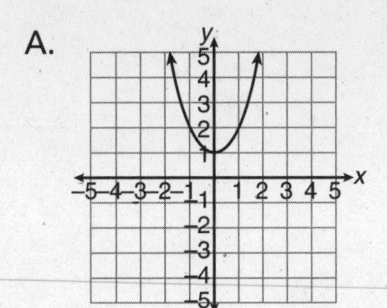

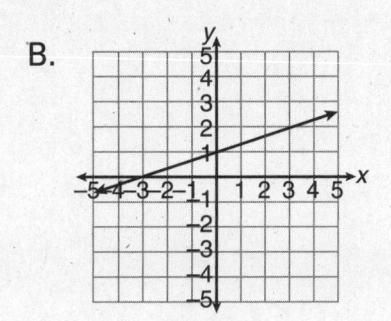

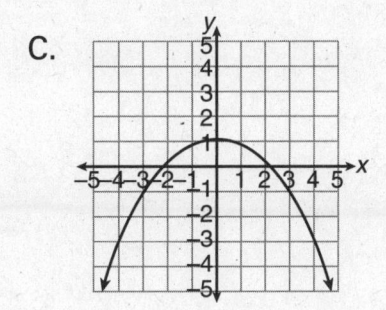

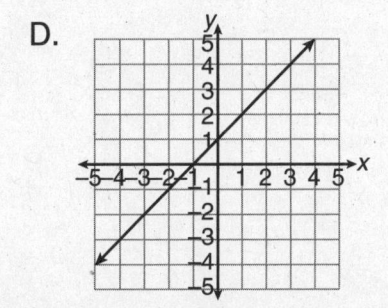

A.

B.

C.

D.

Practice Math OGT 1

Practice Math OGT 2

REFERENCE CHART FOR PRACTICE MATH OGT 2

Area Formulas

parallelogram $\quad A = bh$

rectangle $\quad A = lh$

trapezoid $\quad A = \frac{1}{2}h(b_1 + b_2)$

trapezoid $\quad A = \frac{1}{2}bh$

Circle Formulas

$C = 2\pi r \qquad \pi \approx 3.14 \text{ or } \frac{22}{7}$

$A = 2\pi r^2$

Volume Formulas

cone $\quad V = \frac{1}{2}\pi r^2 h$

cylinder $\quad V = \pi r^2 h$

pyramid $\quad V = \frac{1}{3}Bh \quad B = \text{area of base}$

rectangular prism $\quad V = lwh$

right prism $\quad V = Bh \quad B = \text{area of base}$

sphere $\quad V = \frac{4}{3}\pi r^3$

Combinations

$_nC_r = C(n,r) = \frac{n!}{r(n-r)n!}$

Permutations

$_nP_r = P(n,r) = \frac{n!}{(n-r)!}$

Distance Formula

$d = \sqrt{(x_2 - x_1)^2 + (y_2 - y_1)^2}$

Quadratic Formula

$x = \frac{-b \pm \sqrt{b^2 - 4ac}}{2a}$

Trigonometry

$\sin A = \frac{\text{opposite}}{\text{hypotenuse}}$

$\cos A = \frac{\text{adjacent}}{\text{hypotenuse}}$

$\tan A = \frac{\text{opposite}}{\text{adjacent}}$

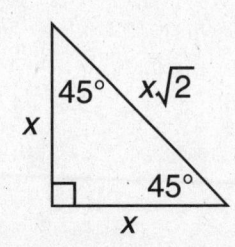

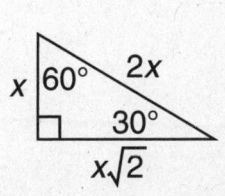

Practice Math OGT 2

ANSWER DOCUMENT FOR PRACTICE MATH OGT 2

1. Ⓐ Ⓑ Ⓒ Ⓓ
2. Ⓐ Ⓑ Ⓒ Ⓓ
3. Ⓐ Ⓑ Ⓒ Ⓓ
4. Ⓐ Ⓑ Ⓒ Ⓓ
5. Ⓐ Ⓑ Ⓒ Ⓓ
6. Ⓐ Ⓑ Ⓒ Ⓓ
7. Four-point extended-response question:

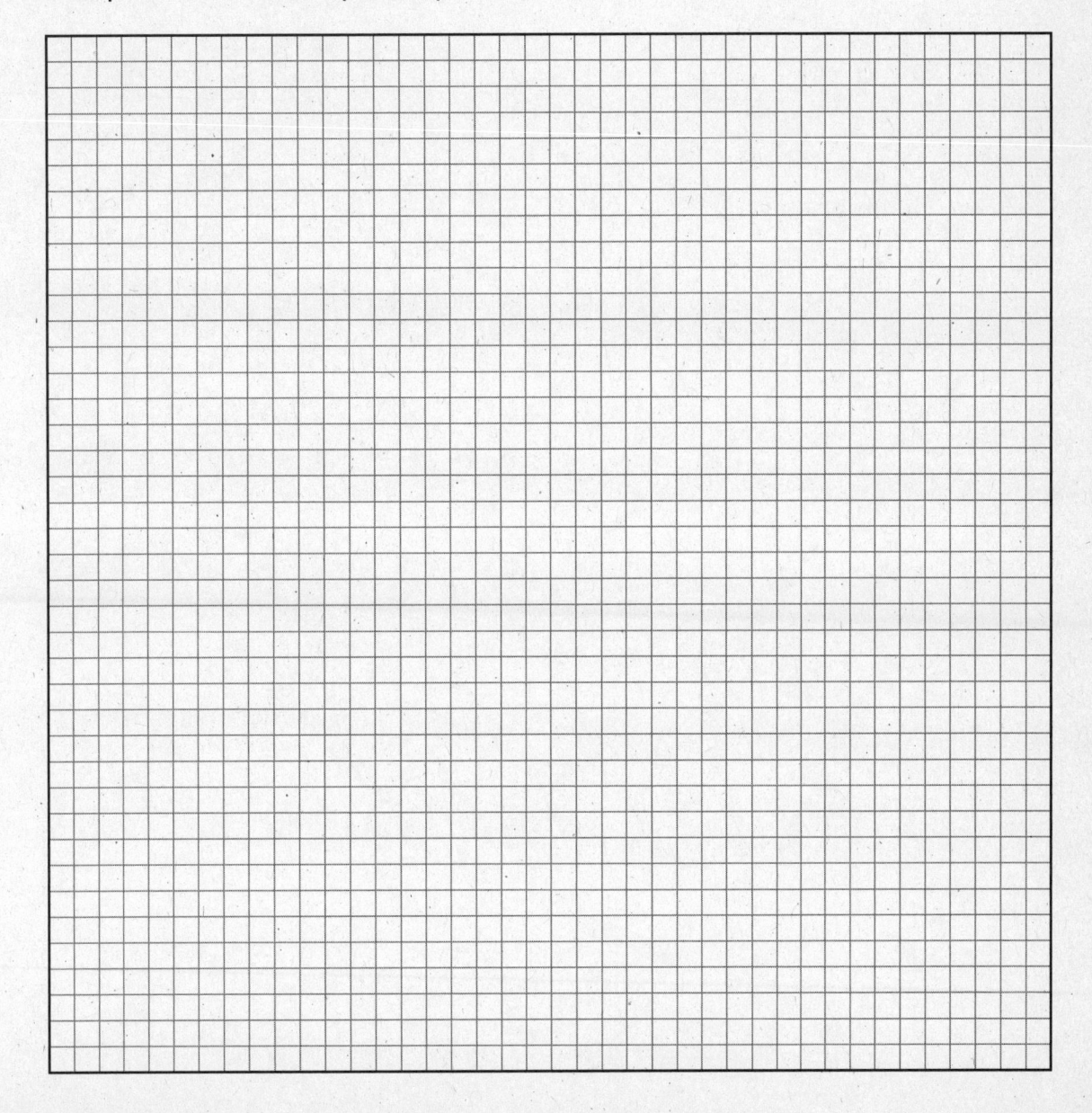

Practice Math OGT 2

8. Ⓐ Ⓑ Ⓒ Ⓓ
9. Ⓐ Ⓑ Ⓒ Ⓓ
10. Ⓐ Ⓑ Ⓒ Ⓓ
11. Ⓐ Ⓑ Ⓒ Ⓓ
12. Ⓐ Ⓑ Ⓒ Ⓓ
13. Ⓐ Ⓑ Ⓒ Ⓓ
14. Ⓐ Ⓑ Ⓒ Ⓓ
15. Ⓐ Ⓑ Ⓒ Ⓓ
16. Ⓐ Ⓑ Ⓒ Ⓓ
17. Ⓐ Ⓑ Ⓒ Ⓓ

18. Four-point extended-response question:

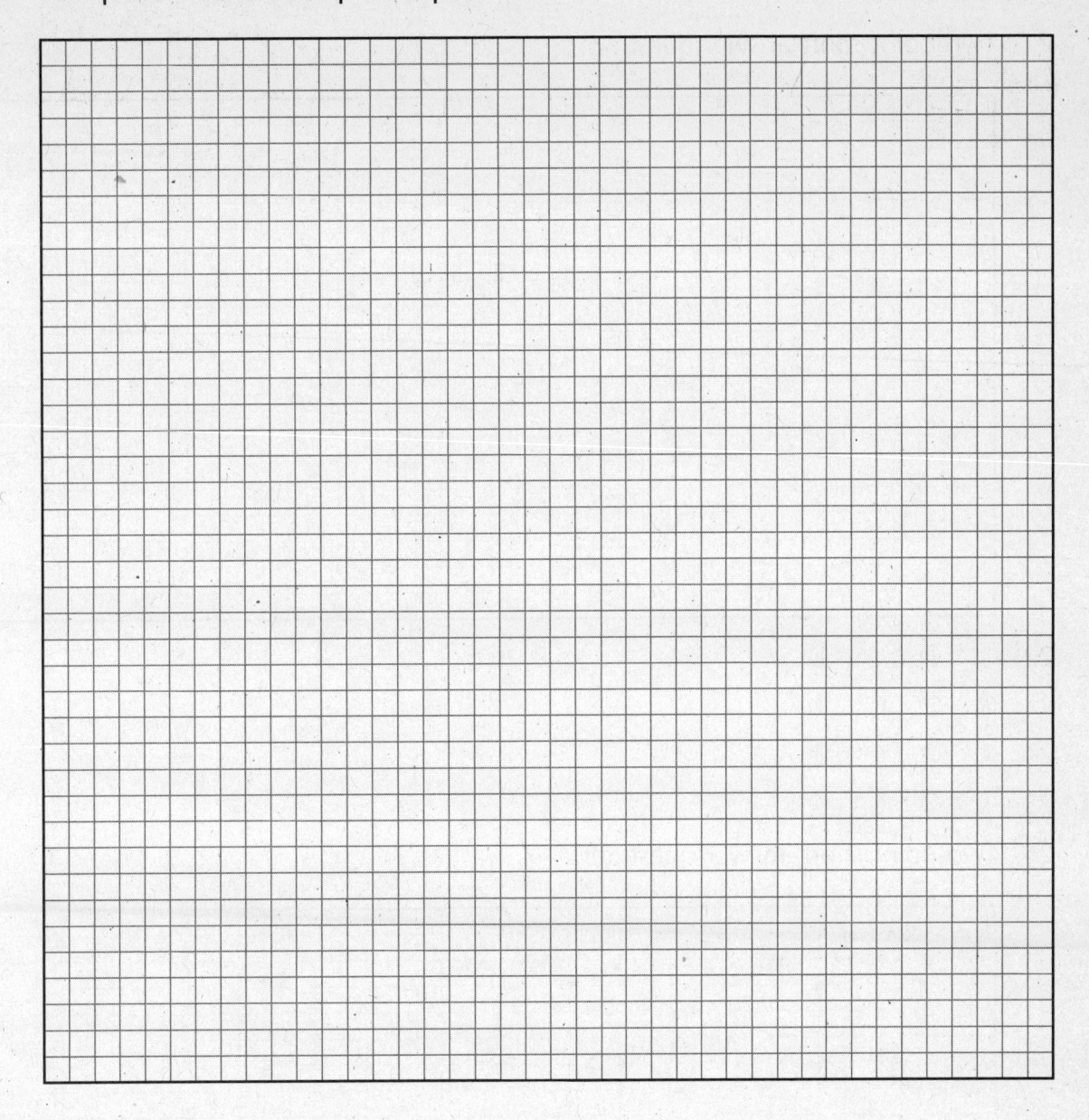

19. Ⓐ Ⓑ Ⓒ Ⓓ
20. Ⓐ Ⓑ Ⓒ Ⓓ
21. Two-point short-answer question:

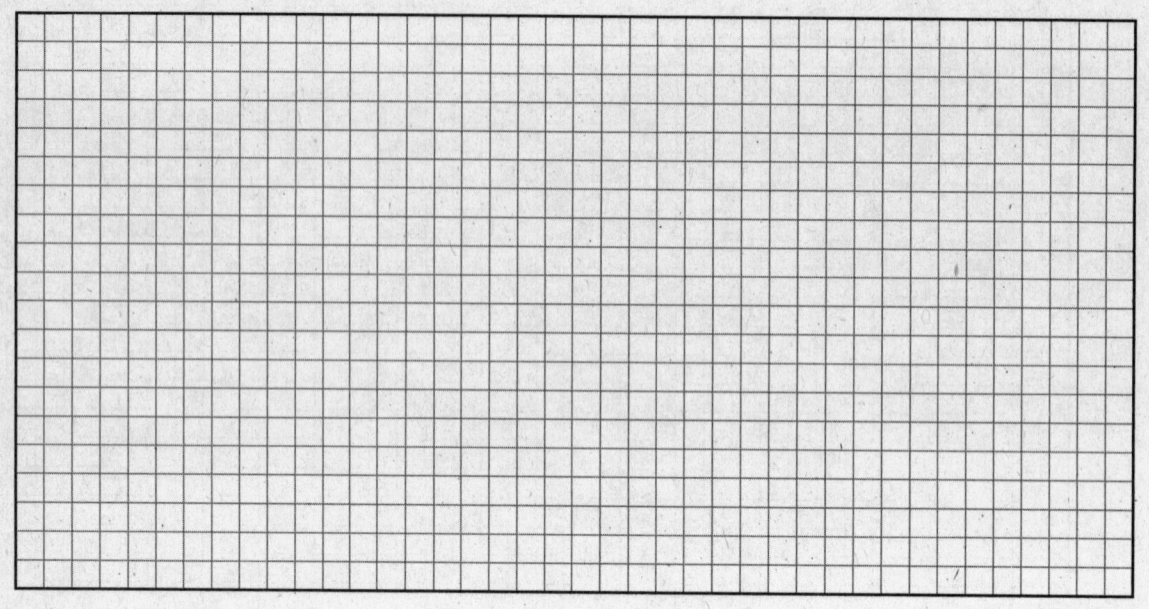

22. Ⓐ Ⓑ Ⓒ Ⓓ
23. Ⓐ Ⓑ Ⓒ Ⓓ
24. Ⓐ Ⓑ Ⓒ Ⓓ
25. Ⓐ Ⓑ Ⓒ Ⓓ
26. Two-point short-answer question:

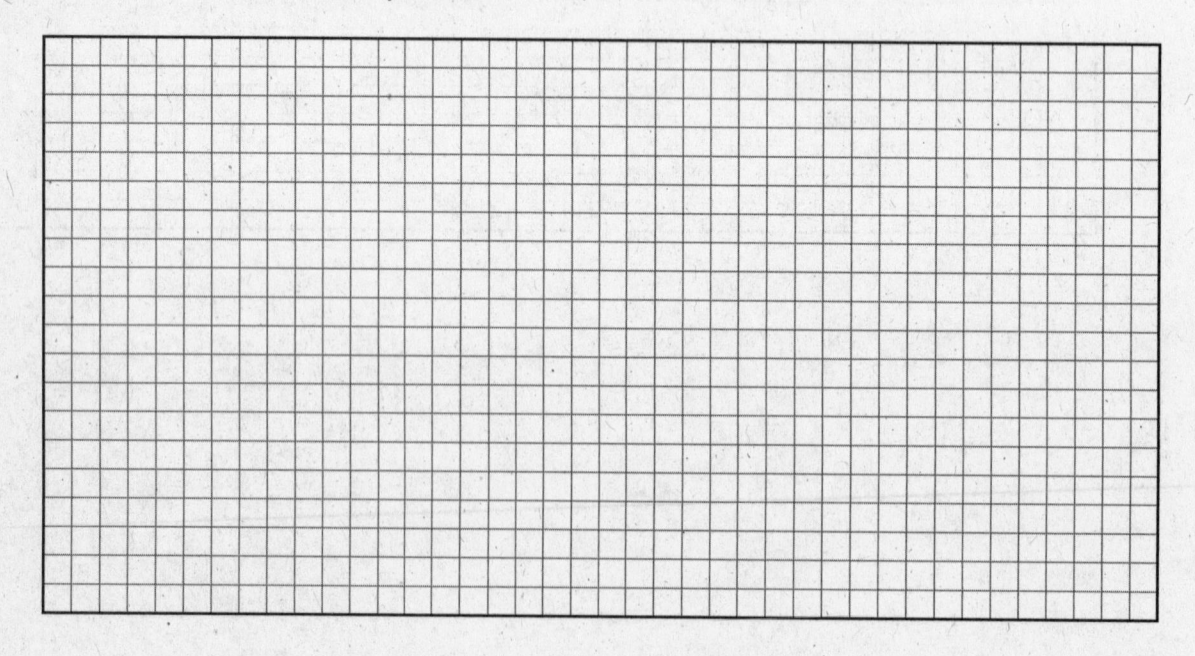

27. Ⓐ Ⓑ Ⓒ Ⓓ
28. Ⓐ Ⓑ Ⓒ Ⓓ
29. Ⓐ Ⓑ Ⓒ Ⓓ
30. Ⓐ Ⓑ Ⓒ Ⓓ
31. Ⓐ Ⓑ Ⓒ Ⓓ
32. Ⓐ Ⓑ Ⓒ Ⓓ
33. Ⓐ Ⓑ Ⓒ Ⓓ
34. Two-point short-answer question:

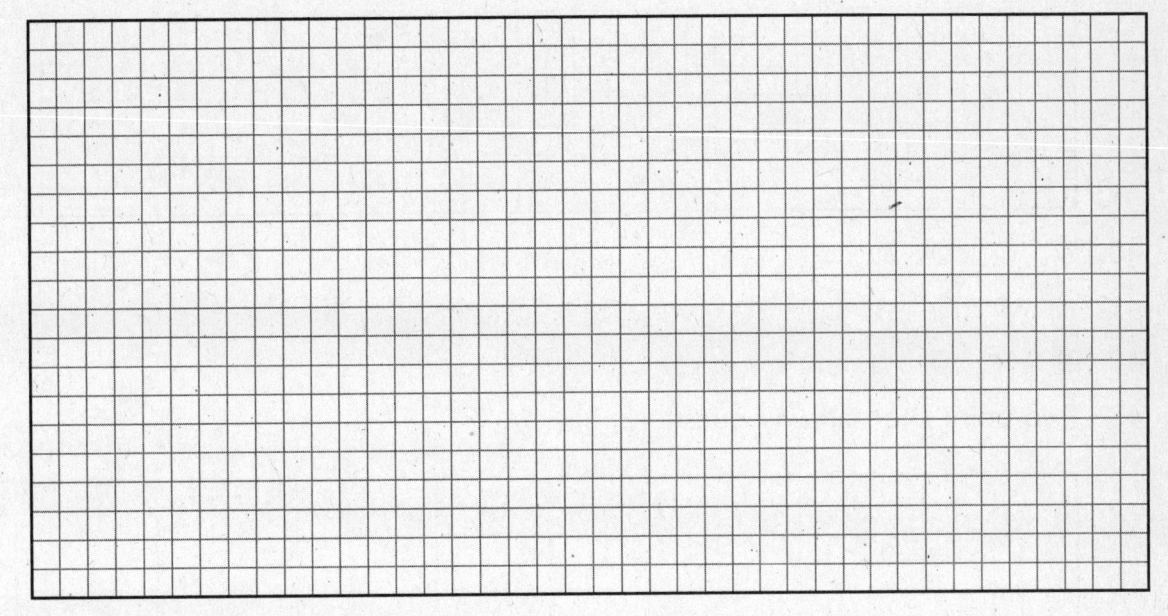

35. Ⓐ Ⓑ Ⓒ Ⓓ
36. Ⓐ Ⓑ Ⓒ Ⓓ
37. Ⓐ Ⓑ Ⓒ Ⓓ
38. Ⓐ Ⓑ Ⓒ Ⓓ

Practice Math OGT 2

39. Two-point short-answer question:

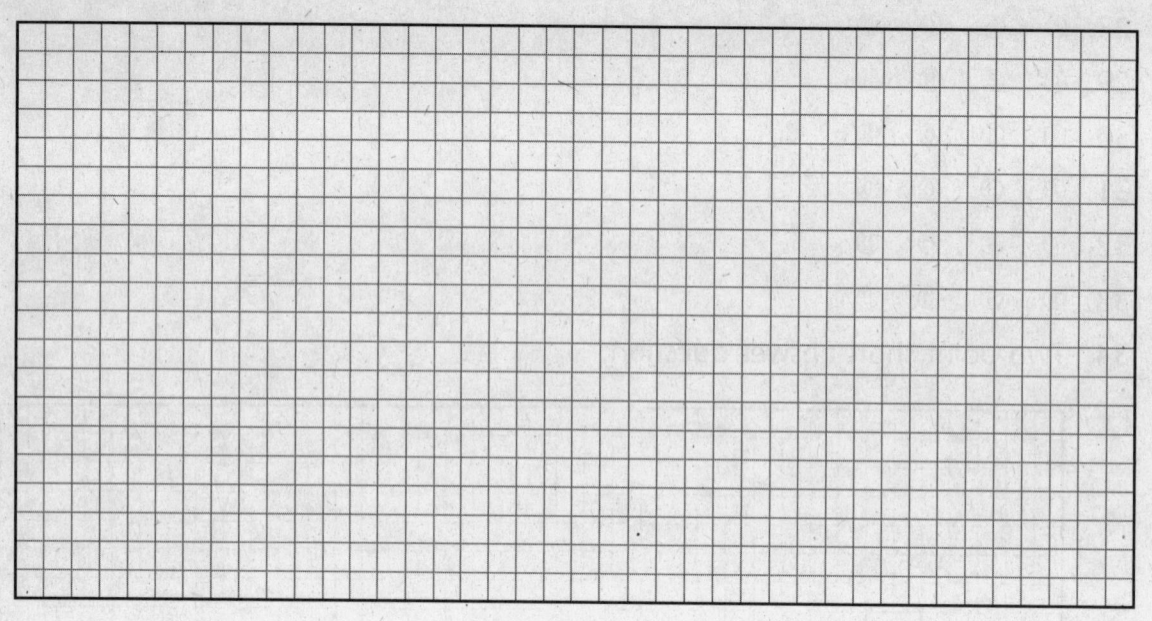

40. Ⓐ Ⓑ Ⓒ Ⓓ
41. Ⓐ Ⓑ Ⓒ Ⓓ
42. Ⓐ Ⓑ Ⓒ Ⓓ
43. Two-point short-answer question:

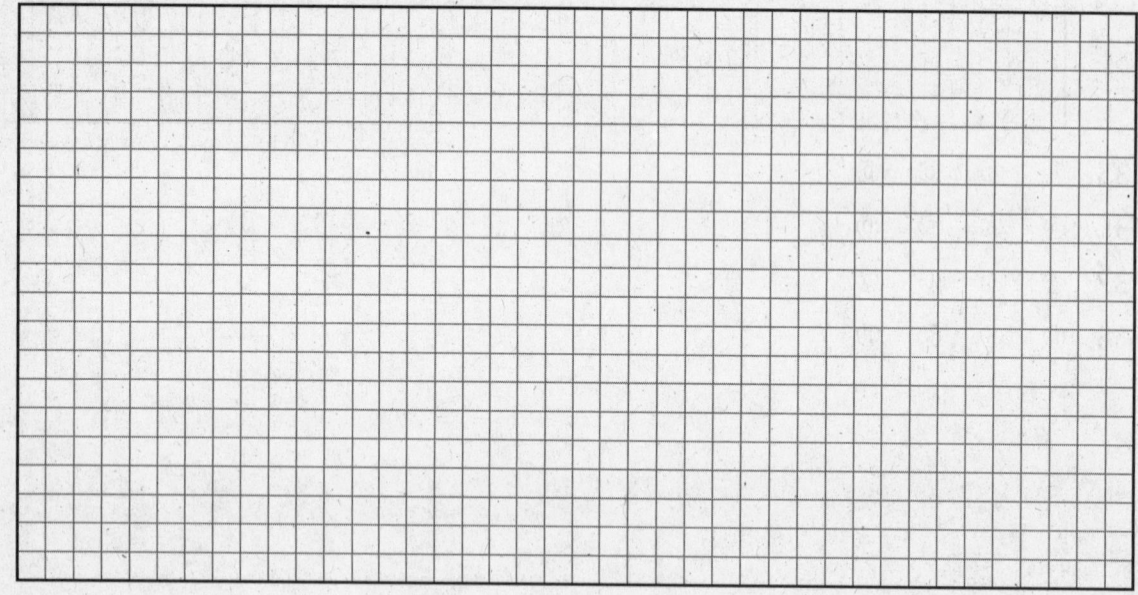

44. Ⓐ Ⓑ Ⓒ Ⓓ

PRACTICE MATH OGT 2

Directions: The practice math OGT contains 44 questions: 37 multiple-choice questions, 5 short-answer questions, and 2 extended-response questions. When answering the multiple-choice questions, solve each problem and then fill in the correct answer choice on the Answer Document. When answering the short-answer and extended-response questions, be sure that you answer completely and that all of your work is contained in the Answer Document. *Only the Answer Document will be scored.*

---

1. Leti is decorating her rectangular bedroom, and she wants to trim it with a string of lights. She decided that two strings of lights that are each 8 feet long and two strings of lights that are 12 feet long will be able to cover the distance around the room. The distance around Leti's room is 38 feet. Which could the dimensions of Leti's room be if one set of lights goes on each wall?

   A. 6 feet by 14 feet
   B. 7 feet by 12 feet
   C. 8 feet by 12 feet
   D. 9 feet by 10 feet

2. To raise money, the senior class is renting a Ferris wheel to operate at the county fair. It costs $260 to rent the Ferris wheel. The senior class will charge $2.50 per ride. Which inequality should the senior class use to find out how many rides, r, it needs to sell to make a profit of at least $470?

   A. $2.5r - 260 \geq 470$
   B. $2.5r + 260 \leq 470$
   C. $2.5r - 260 \leq 470$
   D. $2.5r + 260 \geq 470$

Go to next page

3. Hasid and his work friends went out for lunch at Harry's on Main Street.

Harry's Lunch Menu
Fries.................. $2.60
Onion Rings....... $3.10
BLT.................... $6.25
Burger............... $7.00
Tuna Melt........... $6.50

Soda.................. $1.50
Coffee............... $0.95

Hasid and his five friends ordered three orders of fries, two orders of onion rings, and six tuna melts. Everyone had a soda.

How much will the bill be if the sales tax is 7%?

A. $58.74
B. $61.80
C. $66.34
D. $68.92

4. A rocket-powered race car used a parachute to help stop its momentum. After the parachute ejected, the car traveled 1,050 feet before it stopped. It took the car one minute and 45 seconds to stop.

What was the race car's rate of stopping, in feet per second, from the time the parachute ejected to the time when the car stopped?

A. 2 feet per second
B. 5 feet per second
C. 10 feet per second
D. 12 feet per second

Go to next page

5. Velocity is a measure of the distance an object travels in a certain amount of time.

$$\text{velocity} = \frac{\text{distance}}{\text{time}}$$

How does velocity change as time decreases?

A. The velocity decreases.
B. The velocity increases.
C. The velocity stays the same.
D. The velocity increases and decreases over time.

6. The box-and-whisker plot below represents last year's 10th-grade math scores.

10th Grade Math Scores

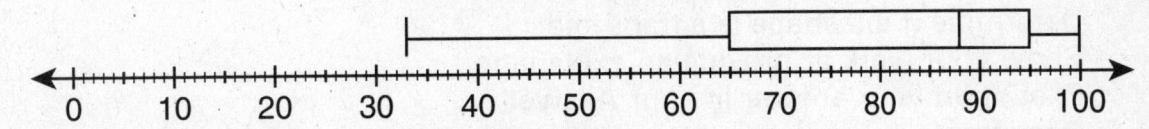

Which of these is the range of their test scores?

A. 33
B. 60.5
C. 67
D. 88

Go to next page

Practice Math OGT 2

7. Four points are connected with line segments on the coordinate plane below.

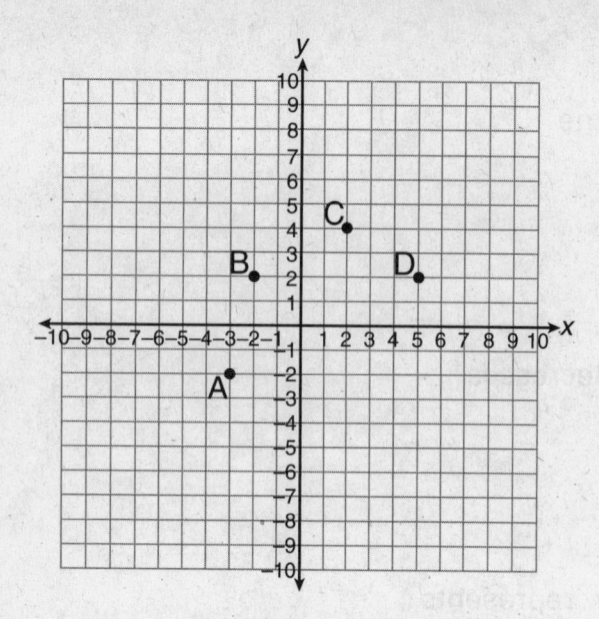

For question number 7, use the separate **Answer Document** for your complete response. This question is worth 4 points.

[Coordinate plane showing points: B at approximately (-3, 2), C at (2, 4), D at (5, 2), A at (-2, -2)]

Find the slope of $\overline{AD}$ and $\overline{BC}$. Write your answer in your **Answer Document**.

Determine if the shape is a trapezoid. Show your work or provide an explanation to support your answer in your **Answer Document**.

Go to next page

198 Roadmap to the Ohio Graduation Test: Mathematics

8. An American car company produced different types of automobiles in the quantities listed below.

American Car Company Production

Car	Number Produced
convertible	$\frac{120,000}{100}$
minivan	one hundred thousand
compact car	1.2 million
SUV	1.02×10^5

Which of the following lists the cars in order from the least to greatest by the number of cars produced?

A. compact car, SUV, minivan, convertible
B. convertible, minivan, SUV, compact car
C. convertible, SUV, minivan, compact car
D. compact car, convertible, SUV, minivan

9. The mean of Hansel's two math test scores was 93%. On his next three math tests, he received 85%, 94%, and 70%. What is the mean score of Hansel's math tests?

A. 82%
B. 85%
C. 87%
D. 89%

Go to next page

Practice Math OGT 2

10. A circle is sketched on a coordinate plane with the center at (3, 4). The circle passes through the point (−2, −1). Which of these expressions could be used to find r, the radius of the circle?

   A. $\sqrt{(3+2)^2+(4+1)^2}$

   B. $\sqrt{(2+3)^2+(1+4)^2}$

   C. $\sqrt{(3-2)^2+(4-1)^2}$

   D. $\sqrt{(2-3)^2+(1-4)^2}$

11. On the number line below, which letter best represents $\sqrt{20}$?

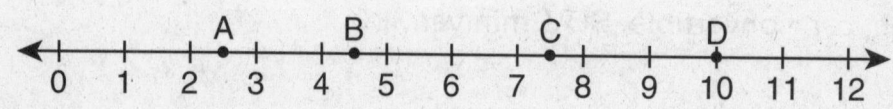

   A. A
   B. B
   C. C
   D. D

Go to next page

12. Jorge is standing 100 feet away from a tall building. The angle of elevation from Jorge's feet to the top of the building is 84.5°.

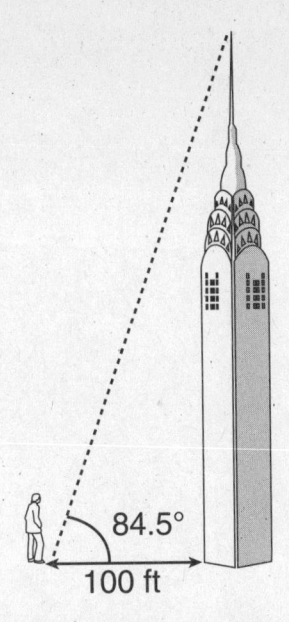

84.5°
100 ft

What is the approximate height of the skyscraper?

A. 57 feet
B. 100 feet
C. 519 feet
D. 1,039 feet

13. Heather bought a sweater that was originally $38 and was on sale for 15% off. A sales tax of 8% was added.

How much did Heather pay for the sweater?

A. $29.65
B. $32.30
C. $34.88
D. $41.04

Go to next page

Practice Math OGT 2

14. The Venn diagram represents relationships between three different kinds of triangles.

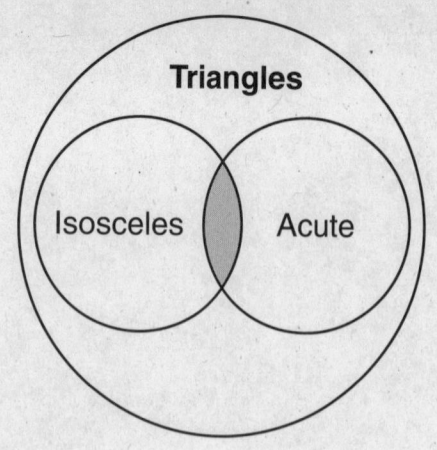

Triangles
Isosceles | Acute

Which of the following triangles belongs in the shaded region of the diagram?

A. Triangle with angles 100°, 40°, 40°

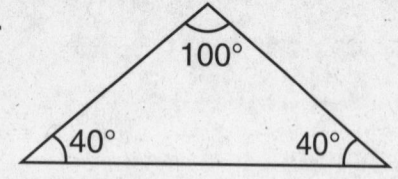

B. Triangle with angles 30°, 75°, 75°

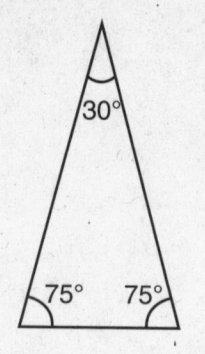

C. Right triangle with angles 45°, 45°

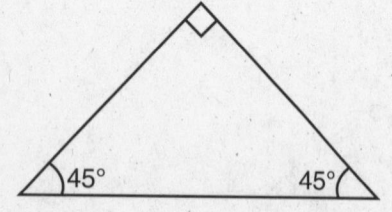

D. Triangle with angles 30°, 120°, 25°

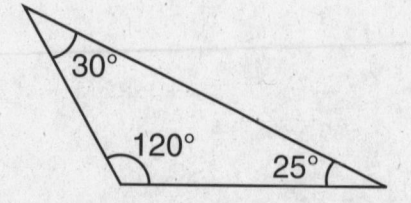

Go to next page

15. Below are two similar triangles.

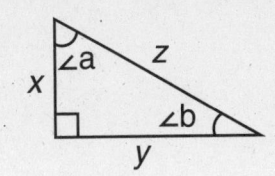

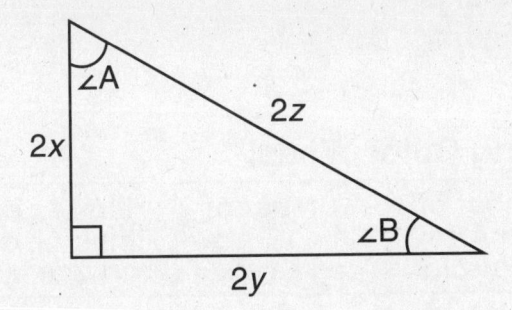

If ∠a is 32°, what is the measure of ∠A?

A. 16°
B. 32°
C. 64°
D. 72°

Practice Math OGT 2

16. Alexis, Matthew, and Rachael took turns spinning an arrow mounted on a wheel, which was divided into 10 equal sections. Each section was painted white, purple, black, or green. Each time the arrow stopped on a section, they recorded the color of the section. Below is a table that shows how many times each person spun the arrow and what the results were.

Results of Spinning Color Wheel

Name	Number of Spins	Number of Times Arrow on White	Number of Times Arrow on Purple	Number of Times Arrow on Black	Number of Times Arrow on Green
Alexis	20	5	9	3	3
Matthew	30	5	16	3	6
Rachael	40	8	20	5	7

Based on this outcome, if Jacob took a turn and spun the arrow 60 times, which of the answer choices below shows the most likely number of times the arrow will land on the white section, the purple section, the black section, and the green section?

A. white = 8, purple = 29, black = 11, green = 12

B. white = 8, purple = 12, black = 29, green = 11

C. white = 11, purple = 8, black = 12, green = 29

D. white = 11, purple = 29, black = 8, green = 12

Go to next page

Roadmap to the Ohio Graduation Test: Mathematics

17. Which of the expressions below is equivalent to $(x^4) \times (3x^2) \times (2x^2)$?

   A. $5x^7$

   B. $6x^8$

   C. $6x^{16}$

   D. $8x^6$

For question number 18, use the separate **Answer Document** for your complete response. This question is worth 4 points.

18. The winning times for the women's Olympic 100-meter dash between the years 1928 and 1980 is shown in the table below.

Women's Olympic 100-meter Dash Winning Times

Year	Time
1928	12.20
1932	11.90
1936	11.50
1948	11.90
1952	11.50
1956	11.50
1960	11.00
1964	11.40
1968	11.00
1972	11.00
1976	11.00
1980	11.00
1984	10.90

Use an appropriate graph to display the data in your **Answer Document**. Then, tell why you used that particular type of graph.

Go to next page

Practice Math OGT 2

19. The Walkers have just built a rectangular porch with a circular terrace that they want to enclose with a railing.

The Walkers' New Porch and Terrace

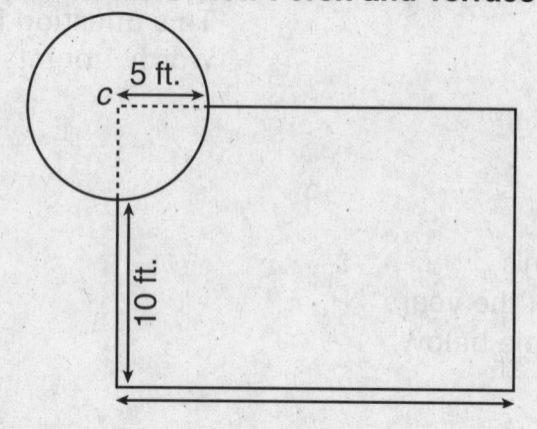

To the nearest foot, what is the minimum length of railing that the Walkers will need to fully surround the porch and terrace?

A. 19 feet
B. 24 feet
C. 42 feet
D. 66 feet

20. Rachael found a new part-time job. She owns 3 pairs of shoes, 3 skirts, and 5 blouses. How many days can Rachael go without wearing the same outfit twice?

   A. 11
   B. 38
   C. 45
   D. 52

For question number 21, use the separate **Answer Document** for your complete response. This question is worth 2 points.

21. The dots in the figures below form a pattern.

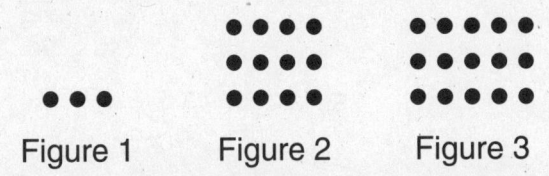

   Figure 1   Figure 2   Figure 3

   In your **Answer Document**, write an algebraic expression for the number of dots in the nth figure.

   Based on the algebraic expression you have written, find the number of dots that would make up Figure 20.

Go to next page

Practice Math OGT 2

22. The diameter of a human hair can range from 17 to 181 micrometers. One meter is equal to one million micrometers. What is the range of one strand of human hair in meters?

A. from 0.000017 meters to 0.000181 meters

B. from 1.7×10^{-3} meters to 1.81×10^{-4}

C. from $\dfrac{17}{10,000}$ meters to $\dfrac{181}{100,000}$ meters

D. from $\dfrac{17}{1,000}$ meters to $\dfrac{181}{1,000}$ meters

Go to next page

23. Seventh-grade students who score above an 80 on a year-end math test are placed in the Algebra I class for eighth grade. The graph shows the number of students who got certain scores.

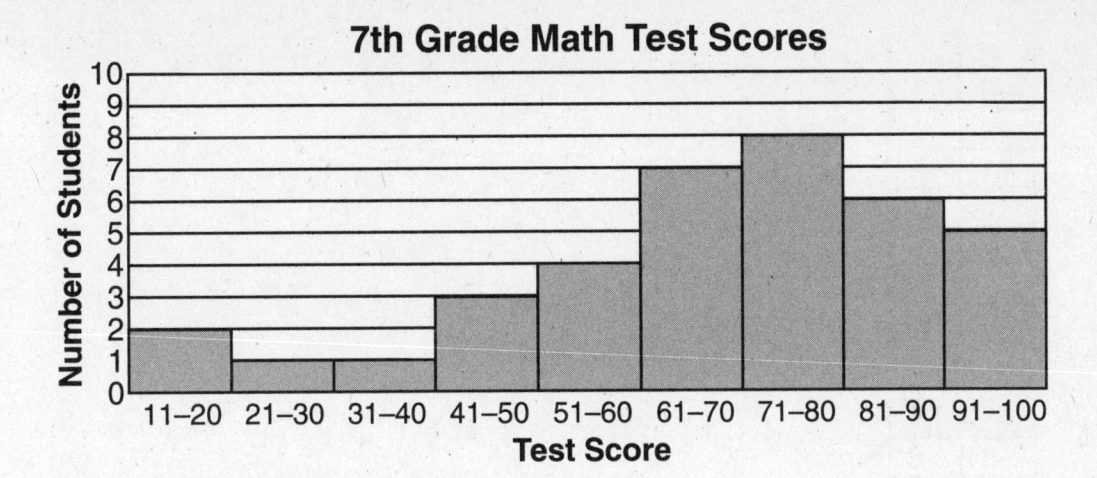

7th Grade Math Test Scores

(Bar graph — Number of Students vs Test Score:
11–20: 2; 21–30: 1; 31–40: 1; 41–50: 3; 51–60: 4; 61–70: 7; 71–80: 8; 81–90: 6; 91–100: 5)

According to the graph, how many students scored above an 80 on the math test?

A. 6
B. 8
C. 11
D. 19

24. Juan will make $1,625 from a part-time job. He can use the equation $y = -2.5x + 1,625$, where x is the number of times he takes the bus to work for $2.50 per ride and y is the $1,475 he wants to save as a deposit on a car. How many times he can take the bus and still leave himself enough for the car deposit?

A. 35
B. 40
C. 60
D. 75

Go to next page

Practice Math OGT 2

209

25. For homework, Dwayne has to graph the parabola represented by the equation $y = x^2 + 1$. Which one of the following tables lists the correct y-values for the given x-values?

A.

x	y
−3	9
−2	4
−1	1
0	0
1	1
2	4
3	9

B.

x	y
−3	−8
−2	−3
−1	0
0	1
1	2
2	5
3	10

C.

x	y
−3	−10
−2	−5
−1	−2
0	1
1	2
2	5
3	10

D.

x	y
−3	10
−2	5
−1	2
0	1
1	2
2	5
3	10

Go to next page

26. The table below shows the number of hours three students spent watching television over a four-week period.

Number of Hours Spent Watching TV

	Week 1	Week 2	Week 3	Week 4
Tricia	15	18	13	20
José	9	12	11	14
Rosa	11	13	8	12

Determine the mean for each student. Then, find the mean for the entire set of data. Show your answers and all your work in your **Answer Document**.

For question number 26, use the separate **Answer Document** for your complete response. This question is worth 2 points.

Go to next page

27. Below is a table showing a moving object's displacement from its initial position over time.

t time in seconds	d displacement in meters
1	0
2	6
3	11
4	18
5	27

Which of the equations below describes d, the displacement in meters of the moving object from its initial position, according to t, the time in seconds?

A. $d = t - 2$
B. $d = t + 2$
C. $d = t^2 - 2$
D. $d = t^2 + 2$

28. The graph below shows the percentage of married homeowners who put the house in the man's name as opposed to the percentage of married homeowners who put the house in the woman's name.

Married - Couple Homeowners by Gender

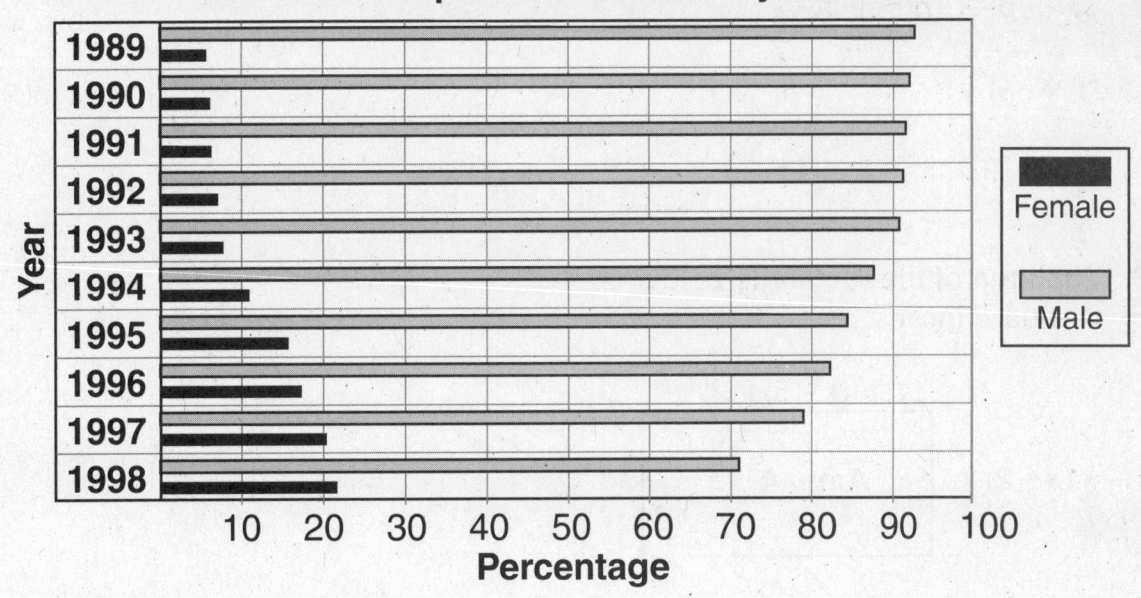

[Bar graph showing Female and Male percentages by Year from 1989 to 1998, with Male percentages decreasing from about 92% to 70% and Female percentages increasing from about 3% to 22%.]

Which of the following statements is true based on the graph?

A. Financial responsibility has always been evenly divided.

B. The male population has decreased.

C. Women are gradually taking more financial responsibility.

D. By the year 2007, the male and female graphs will be the same.

Go to next page

Practice Math OGT 2

29. Which of the following expressions is true?

   A. $(-p) \times (r) = |(-p) \times r|$

   B. $(-p) \times (r) = |-pr|$

   C. $(-p) \times (r) = |-p(-r)|$

   D. $(-p) \times (r) = -|(-p) \times r|$

30. The area of the rectangle below is 4 square inches.

    $(x-2)$ in. | $(x-5)$ in., Area = 4 in.^{2}

    What must be the value of x?

    A. 1
    B. 3
    C. 6
    D. 7

Go to next page

Roadmap to the Ohio Graduation Test: Mathematics

31. Damien collected pennies over several years and put them into a jar. Once the jar was full, he removed all the pennies from the jar. From those pennies, Damien had placed 55% of them into a bank account, he spent 0.25 of them, and he gave his brother $\frac{1}{10}$ of them. What percent of pennies is left from the original full jar?

A. 10%
B. 12%
C. 15%
D. 20%

Go to next page

Practice Math OGT 2

32. The relationship between an object's density and its volume is described by the equation density = $\frac{mass}{volume}$. Which graph represents this equation, assuming the mass stays constant?

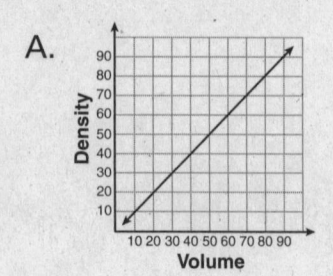

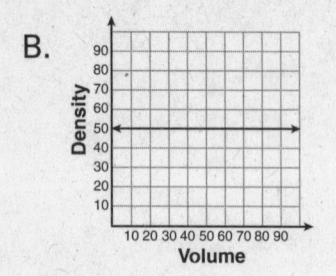

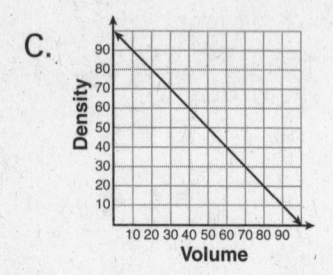

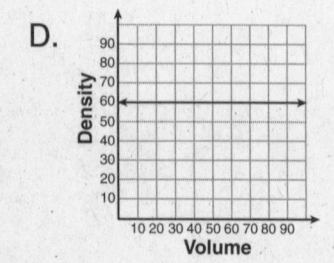

A.

B.

C.

D.

33. For which of the polyhedra below is the volume formula $V = lwh$ applicable, where V is the volume, l is the length of its base, w is the length of the width, and h the height of the polyhedra?

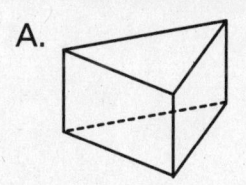

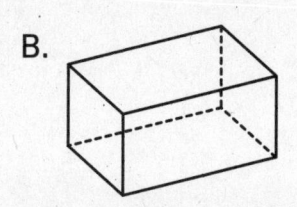

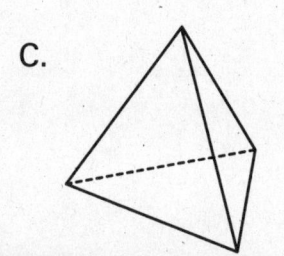

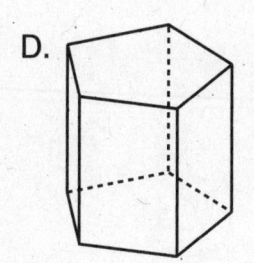

A.

B.

C.

D.

Go to next page

Practice Math OGT 2

34. A juice company had a gross income of $1,220,342.40. The company determined that 423,730 people had purchased their juice. This meant that each person spent $2.88 per juice.

    Write, in your **Answer Document**, how a different juice company could have 211,865 people buy their juice—but have the same gross income.

For question number 34, use the separate **Answer Document** for your complete response. This question is worth 2 points.

35. Natasha bought a pencil case as well as a set of colored pencils. Below are the dimensions of one pencil. Which box will be large enough to fit all her pencils if a set contains 30?

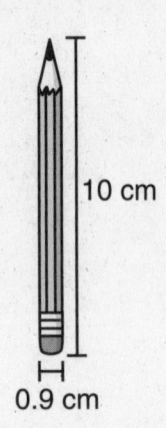

    10 cm

    0.9 cm

    A. 9 centimeters × 9 centimeters × 3 centimeters
    B. 9 centimeters × 6 centimeters × 3 centimeters
    C. 12 centimeters × 6 centimeters × 4 centimeters
    D. 12 centimeters × 9 centimeters × 3 centimeters

Go to next page

36. Patricia makes gift items and ships them to customers. She uses shredded paper to fill the shipping containers shown below.

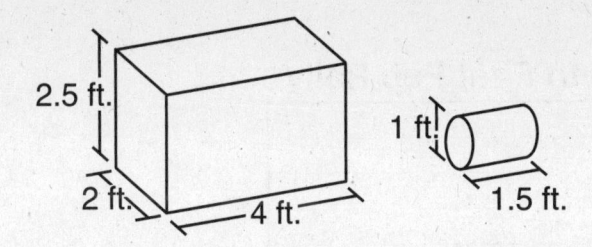

If the box and the tube contained only shredded paper, approximately how many tubes would contain the same amount of shredded paper as one box?

A. 6
B. 8
C. 12
D. 17

37. Center High School just held its first pep rally. The math club counted how many members of each class decided to come. The graph shows the totals.

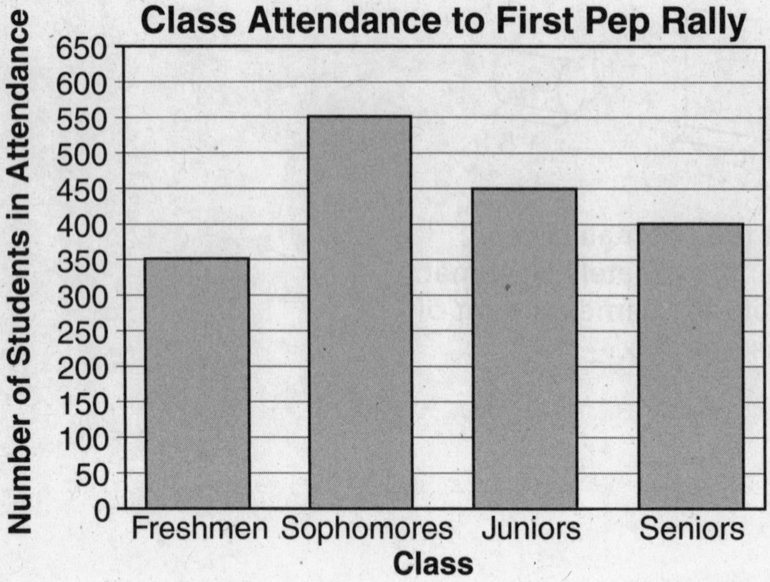

About what percentage of the audience consisted of seniors?

A. 20%

B. 23%

C. 26%

D. 31%

Go to next page

38. Jerome swam across a river 40 feet wide. He intended to swim straight across, and he was surprised to find himself 25 feet down stream due to the strong current.

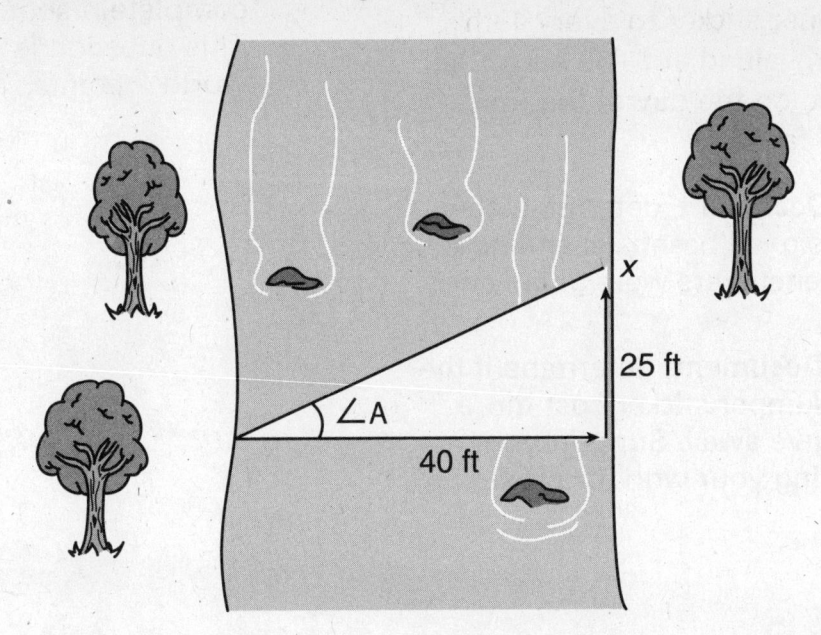

Which of the following equations must be true of Jerome's displacement, ∠A, from his intended destination?

A. $\tan A = \dfrac{25}{40}$

B. $\tan A = \dfrac{40}{25}$

C. $\sin A = \dfrac{25}{40}$

D. $\sin A = \dfrac{40}{25}$

Go to next page

Practice Math OGT 2

39. The Tri-Village Baseball League had a promotion to kick off the season. To every 25th paying customer, they gave a team-signed baseball, valued at $3.99 each. They also gave a bumper sticker to every 10th paying customer, valued at $1.50 each. The stands were filled on the day of the first game with 5,726 fans.

In your **Answer Document**, determine how many free team-signed baseballs and how many free bumper stickers were given away.

In your **Answer Document**, determine if the baseball or the bumper sticker cost more for the team to give away. Support your answer by showing your work or providing an explanation.

For question number 39, use the separate **Answer Document** for your complete response. This question is worth 2 points.

Go to next page

40. The quadrilateral EVOL has vertices at the coordinates (0, 7), (2, 8), (4, 6), and (0, 1), as shown.

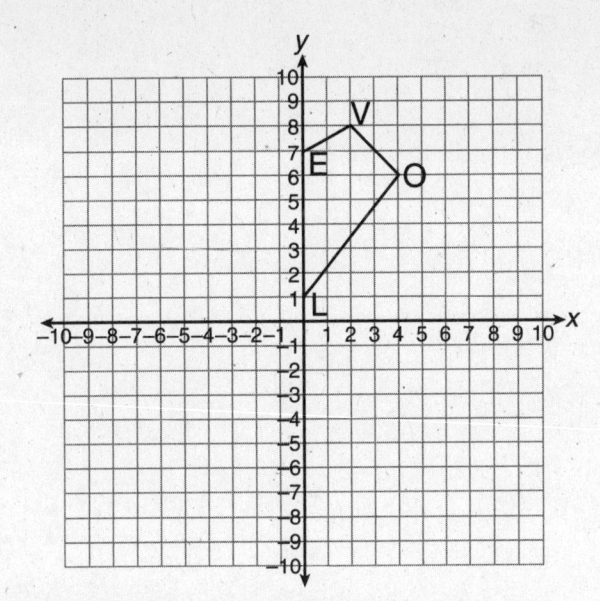

What are the coordinates of the vertices of quadrilateral EVOL when it is reflected over the y-axis?

A. (0, 7), (2, 8), (4, 6), (0, 1)
B. (0, −7), (2, −8), (4, −6), (0, −1)
C. (0, 7), (−2, 8), (−4, 6), (0, 1)
D. (0, −7), (−2, −8), (−4, −6), (0, −1)

Go to next page

Practice Math OGT 2

223

41. Which pair of equations represents lines that are parallel and perpendicular, respectively, to the graph of $y = -\frac{5}{8}x + 6$?

A. $y = -\frac{5}{8}x + 5$ and $y = -\frac{8}{5}x + 4$

B. $y = -\frac{5}{8}x + 9$ and $y = \frac{8}{5}x + 3$

C. $y = \frac{5}{8}x + 7$ and $y = -\frac{5}{8}x + 1$

D. $y = \frac{5}{8}x + 4$ and $y = \frac{5}{8}x + 5$

Go to next page

42. A map of Dayton, Ohio, shows Mayfair Road, Rustic Road, and Emerson Avenue as parallel streets running north and south. West Fairview Avenue diagonally intersects those streets.

Dayton, Ohio Street Map

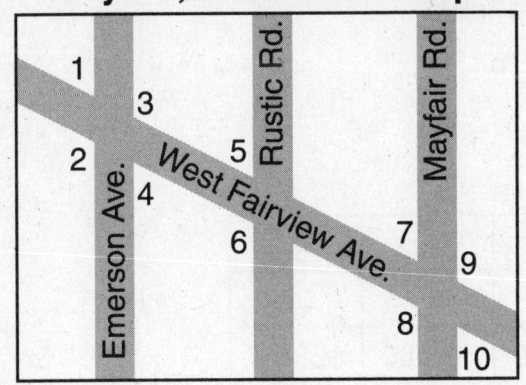

If all of the streets are perfectly straight, which pair of angles is congruent?

A. ∠1 and ∠3
B. ∠2 and ∠5
C. ∠3 and ∠6
D. ∠4 and ∠8

For question number 43, use the separate **Answer Document** for your complete response. This question is worth 2 points.

Go to next page

Practice Math OGT 2

43. Bonnie made $6.00 per hour waiting tables. The owner of the restaurant agreed to pay her $1\frac{1}{2}$ times her hourly wage for each hour she worked over 30 hours per week. She kept her tips but was taxed on her hourly income at 12% of her gross pay. The table shows Bonnie's work time and tips for one week.

Bonnie's Hours

Day	Sun.	Tues.	Wed.	Thurs.	Sat.
Hours	$7\frac{1}{2}$	$5\frac{3}{4}$	6	$5\frac{1}{4}$	$9\frac{1}{2}$
Tips	$53.50	$25.75	$33.00	$34.50	$68.75

Determine the amount of pay that Bonnie took home, after taxes are withheld and including tips, for the week shown in the table. Show your work or provide an explanation to support your answer in your **Answer Document**.

Go to next page

44. The clock below shows that the time is 4:00.

What is the approximate measure of the central angle that is created between the hour hand and the minute hand?

A. 20°
B. 33.3°
C. 90°
D. 120°

Practice Math OGT 2

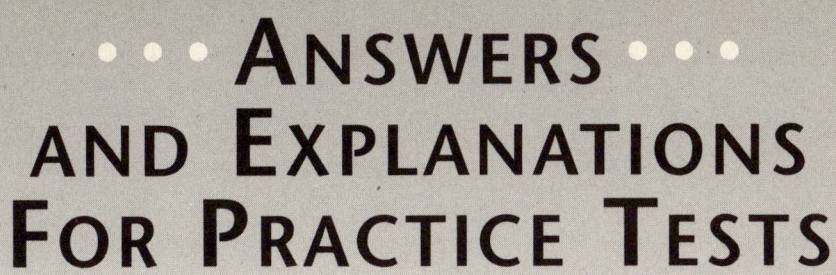

Answers and Explanations for Practice Tests

Answers and Explanations for Practice Math OGT 1

ANSWERS AND EXPLANATIONS FOR PRACTICE MATH OGT 1

1. **C** Charles is creating a 7-letter code, using the letters A, B, C, D, E, F, and G. The letter A must be the second letter in the code but the other letters can be in any order. Visually, this code must look like this: ___ _A_ ___ ___ ___ ___ ___. The first slot in the code can be any one of remaining six letters. After the first slot is filled, Charles will have 5 letters left to choose from for the third slot. Then he will have 4 remaining letters to choose from for the fourth slot, 3 remaining letters to choose from for the fifth slot, 2 remaining letters to choose from for the sixth slot, and then 1 letter remaining for the last slot. So, the number of possible combinations is $6 \times 5 \times 4 \times 3 \times 2 \times 1 = 720$, which is answer choice **C**.

   Even if you did not know how to perform the combination permutation, perhaps you were able to use Process of Elimination (POE) to get rid of answer choice **A**. There are definitely more than six possible combinations of letters for Charles's code!

2. **D** The formula for the volume of a rectangular prism is $V = lwh$. (You can check your reference sheet to be sure of this.) The volume of the pool is $6\ m \times 12\ m \times 2\ m = 144\ m^3$. But be careful not to pick answer choice **A** because the problem states that it takes 1,000 liters to fill one cubic meter. Therefore, $1{,}000\ \text{liters} \times 144\ m^3 = 144{,}000$ liters, which is answer choice **D**.

3. **B** To answer this question, you first will want to identify the pattern. Row 2 has 2 more squares than Row 1; Row 3 has 4 more squares than Row 2; Row 4 has 8 more squares than Row 3. Row 5, then, will have 16 more squares than Row 4, and Row 6 will have 32 more squares than Row 5. Once you know the pattern, you can find the totals: Row 4 has 17 squares, so Row 5 will have 16 more, or 33 squares. Row 6 will have 32 more squares than Row 5, or $32 + 33 = 65$ total squares. If Row 6 will have 65 squares, then answer choice **B** is correct.

4. **C** You can use POE to find the answer choice that accurately states the information in the graph. Just get rid of the choices that are untrue based on the data in the graph.

   Answer choice **A** says that fifty percent of the students rented less than 5 movies. You can see from the graph that that isn't true because median of the lower quartile isn't below 5. Eliminate answer choice **A**. Answer choice **B** says that the range of the data is 10. The upper extreme of the graph is 15 and the lower extreme is 2, so the range is $15 - 2$, or 13. Eliminate that choice too. Answer choice **C** says that the median of the data is 7. The line segment between the quartiles represents the median. In this box-and-whisker plot, the median line is on the 7. This looks like the right answer but check the last answer choice to be sure. Answer choice **D** says that fifty percent of the students rented more than 10 movies. If half of the students had rented more than 10 movies, the median would have to be placed above 10. It's not. Answer choice **C** is correct.

5. **B** You are asked to find the irrational number from the given values in the answer choices. An irrational number is a number that can't be expressed as $\frac{x}{y}$, where x and y are integers and y does not equal 0. Answer choice **A** is $\sqrt{9}$, which is a rational number, because it can also be expressed as the integer 3. Answer choice **B** is $\sqrt{8}$, which may be the correct answer because it can't be expressed as a repeating or terminal decimal. Check the other answer choices, just to be sure. Answer choice **C** is $0.33\overline{3}$, which is a repeating decimal and is therefore rational. Answer choice **D** is $\frac{2}{3}$, which fits the definition of a rational number and is rational. Answer choice **B** is the correct answer.

6. **D** To solve for the missing points in rectangle ABCD, first determine the coordinates of A and B. A is at (–2, 3) and B is at (6, 3). To form a rectangle, points C and D must be directly above or below points A and B. That means one of the points would have to have an *x*-coordinate of –2 to be either directly above or below point A and another point would need an *x*-coordinate of 6 to be either directly above or below point B. Only answer choices **C** and **D** have an *x*-coordinate of –2. The *y*-coordinate of each of those answer choices would be possible to make a rectangle. However, only answer choice **D** has the second set of coordinates with the *x*-coordinate as 6. You can check your answer to see if the points in answer choice **D** would make a rectangle by plotting the points on a piece of scrap paper. The coordinates (–2, –1) and (6, –1) would make a rectangle. Answer choice **D** is correct.

7. **C** Use POE to find which of the measures of central tendency listed in the answer choices is true. Eliminate the ones that are false. Answer choice **A** says that the mean of the test scores is 89.93. Add the scores and divide the total by the number of exams, 6, to see if this answer is correct. 93 + 88 + 85 + 92 + 89 + 92 = 539 ÷ 6 = $89.8\overline{3}$. That's not right, so you can eliminate it. Answer choice **B** says that the median is 85. Put the scores in order: 85, 88, 89, 92, 92, 93. The median is in between 89 and 92, or 90.5, but it's clearly not 85. Answer choice **B** is incorrect. Answer choice **C** says that the mode is 92. 92 is the score that appears the most often, so this looks like the correct answer. But check answer choice **D** to be sure. Answer choice **D** says that the range is 7. The range is the difference between the highest and lowest values, which is 93 – 85 = 8 in this case. Answer choice **C** is indeed correct.

8. First, be careful to notice the word **not** in the question. You are being asked to find the area of the floor **not** covered by the carpet. To do that you will need to find the area of the floor and the area of the carpet and subtract one from the other. The length of the floor is twice the length of the radius of the circle, or 6 feet × 2 = 12 feet. The area of the floor is found with the formula $A = s^2$, or 12 ft^2 or 144 ft^2. The area of the carpet is found with the formula $A = \pi r^2$, or 3.14 × 6^2 or 3.14 × 36 or 113.04 ft^2. Subtract the area of the carpet from the area of the floor: 144 ft^2 − 113.04 ft^2 = 30.96 square feet.

This question is worth 2 points. You would receive 2 points for your answer if you had shown the work for the area of the floor and the area of the circle, then had subtracted the answers correctly. For instance: $A = 12^2 = 144$. $A = 3.14 \times 6^2 = 3.14 \times 36 = 113.04$. 144 − 113.04 = 30.96 square feet. Remember to use your reference sheet for the formulas.

9. **B** The first step in solving this problem is to find the amount of the final bill. Subtract the $10 discount: $65 − $10 = $55. The girls paid a total of $66, so the tip was the difference of $55 and $66: $66 − $55 = $11. To find the percentage of the tip, you can put the tip over the final bill: $\frac{11}{55}$. You can divide or simplify to $\frac{1}{5}$, which is the same as 0.20, which is equivalent to 20%. The girls left a 20% tip, which is answer choice **B**.

10. **D** To find how much Aleesha would need to earn on the sixth day of babysitting, first find the total of her earning for the five days: $26 + $38 + $20 + $46 + $35 = $165. If she wanted to earn a mean of $35 per day over six days, then the total for the six days would be equal to $35 × 6 = $210. Subtract the amount she earned for five days from the total amount she needs to earn over six days: 210 − 165 = 45. Aleesha would have to earn $45 on the sixth day to earn a mean of $35 per day. To check your answer, add the earnings for all six days and divide by six. 26 + 38 + 20 + 46 + 35 + 45 = 210. 210 ÷ 6 = 35. Answer choice **D** is the correct answer.

11. **B** One way to solve this problem is to plug values into each answer choice to determine which one works. One of the plotted points on the graph is (2, 0). Because the first number in the set represents the *x*-coordinate and the second represents the *y*-coordinate, plugging those values into the answer choice **A** equation would give you 0 = 2 + 2, or 0 ≠ 4. Try the next equation: 0 = 2 − 2, or 0 = 0. Answer choice **B** looks like the correct answer. Try the others to be sure. 0 = 2 + 4, or 0 ≠ 6. Answer choice **C** isn't correct. 0 = 2 − 4, or 0 ≠ −2. Answer choice **D** isn't correct either. Answer choice **B** gives you the only equation that fits this chosen coordinate pair, so it must be the correct choice.

Answers and Explanations for Practice Math OGT 1

12. For this question, you have to expect that the sales for Stephen will be about the same as they were for the previous three months. Then, you can take the information and compare the plans to see which will be the most beneficial for Stephen.

    First, find out how much would be made from the straight 20% commission.

    $$\begin{aligned}\$12{,}500 \times 20\% &= \$2{,}500 \\ \$16{,}000 \times 20\% &= \$3{,}200 \\ \$13{,}000 \times 20\% &= \underline{\$2{,}600} \\ &\ \$8{,}300\end{aligned}$$

    Now find out how much he would make from a $1,000 salary, plus a 10% commission.

    $$\begin{aligned}\$12{,}500 \times 10\% = \$1{,}250 + \$1{,}000 &= \$2{,}250 \\ \$16{,}000 \times 10\% = \$1{,}600 + \$1{,}000 &= \$2{,}600 \\ \$13{,}000 \times 10\% = \$1{,}300 + \$1{,}000 &= \underline{\$2{,}300} \\ &\ \$7{,}150\end{aligned}$$

    Stephen would earn more from the straight commission of 20% on his sales.

    This question is worth 2 points. To earn the full 2 points for this question, you would need to identify the better payment plan and clearly explain your answer. For instance, you could have said: Stephen would earn $8,300 from the 20% commission plan and $7,150 on the salary plus 10% commission plan. Therefore, the 20% straight commission plan would benefit Stephen the most.

13. **D** One way to find the equation that works for all of the values of *x* and *y* is to plug the values into the equations from the answer choices. For example, start with the first values from the coordinate pair (−1, −10). Answer choice **A** would equal −10 = −1 − 12, or −10 = −13. That doesn't work, so cross off answer choice **A**. Next, try the values in Answer choice **B**. −10 = −1^2 + (−1) − 10, which becomes −10 = 1 − 1 − 10, or −10 = −10. That works! But if you try the next set of values, (0, −12), you will get −12 = 0^2 + 0 − 10, or −12 = −10. So answer choice **B** doesn't work after all.

    Using those same values for the equation in answer choice **C**, you will get −12 = −2(0 + 6), or −12 = −12. That looks good, but the next set of values, (1, −12), don't fit the same equation: −12 = −2(1 + 6), or −12 = −14 does not work. Now you know answer choice **D** is probably correct, but check to be sure. Plugging that same set of values into the last equation, y = (x + 3)(x − 4) becomes −12 = (1 + 3)(1 − 4), or −12 = 4 × −3, or −12 = −12. This looks like the right answer choice. Plug in the other values to be sure they all work for the equation in answer choice **D**. They do, so answer choice **D** is correct.

14. To respond to this short-answer question, you need to decide if the survey will offer a random sampling of the community. The class is hoping to show a community support from adults. The supermarket and senior citizen center sites would offer a good sampling of adults in the community. But the high school site is unlikely result in an unbiased survey. After all, students would likely want their voice and opinions heard in the local paper.

    This question is worth 2 points. To receive the full 2 points for this question, your answer might be: The survey sites at the supermarket and senior citizen center would offer a random sampling, but the high school site would likely be biased in their answers. This is because high school students would want to publish their stories.

15. **D** To find the correct expression, take each step to the problem as you would to find the actual answer to the problem. First, you would need to find the number of poems that Thomas did not print: 569 − 394. Then, you would divide that number by the total number of poems or 569 and multiply by 100 to get a percent as the answer. The expression should be $\frac{569-394}{569} \times 100$, which is answer choice **D**.

    To check your answer, you can solve each of the equations and see which one gives you a logical answer. Thomas decided to print well over half of the 569 poems, because he prints 394 of them. You want to find how many weren't printed, so you're looking for an answer that gives you less than 50%. If you solve the first expression, you get about 69%; that's too much. If you solve answer choice **B**, you get 144%. That's not right. Answer choice **C** will result in a negative number so it can't be right either. Answer choice **D** works out to about 31%, which sounds like a logical answer.

16. **A** To find out how many buckets of sand will be needed to fill the sandbox, you first need to find how much sand the sandbox will need. The formula for the volume of a rectangular prism is $V = lwh$, which you can verify on the separate reference sheet. Convert the feet measures to inches so that all the measurements are in the same units, and you'll have 60 inches × 60 inches × 6 inches, or 21,600 cubic inches. Now, you'll need to find the volume of the bucket. The formula for the volume of a cylinder is $V = \pi r^2 h$, which becomes 3.14 × 5 inches^2 × 12 inches = 942 cubic inches. Divide the volume of the sandbox by the volume of the bucket: 21,600 ÷ 942 equals 22.93. It will take 23 buckets of sand to fill the sandbox, which is answer choice **A**.

17. **B** Take each part of the question separately to find the graph that fits all of the information. The first part says that the temperature was about the same for the first two months of the year. Only graph A can be eliminated so far. The next part says that there was a gradual rise in the temperature in June. Graph C can be eliminated because the temperature falls in that graph. Graph D can also be eliminated because the temperature rises quickly after the first two months. That leaves graphs B. Make sure that the graph fits with the other information. The temperatures spike in July and August. Graph B looks good for that. Finally, the temperatures gradually got cooler through to December. Graph B looks good for that change too. The correct answer choice is **B**.

18. **D** Two six-sided number cubes have 36 possible outcomes, because $6 \times 6 = 36$. If you look at the table, you can see all 36 outcomes. You want to know how many times the two number cubes will have a sum that equals 7. Count the times that the number 7 appears in the table. It shows up six times, $6 + 1, 5 + 2, 3 + 4, 4 + 3, 5 + 2,$ and $6 + 3$. Because six out of a possible 36 outcomes results in the number you are looking for, that ratio is your answer. And because $\frac{6}{36}$ reduces to $\frac{1}{6}$, answer choice **D** is correct.

19. The correctly drawn triangles should look like the following:

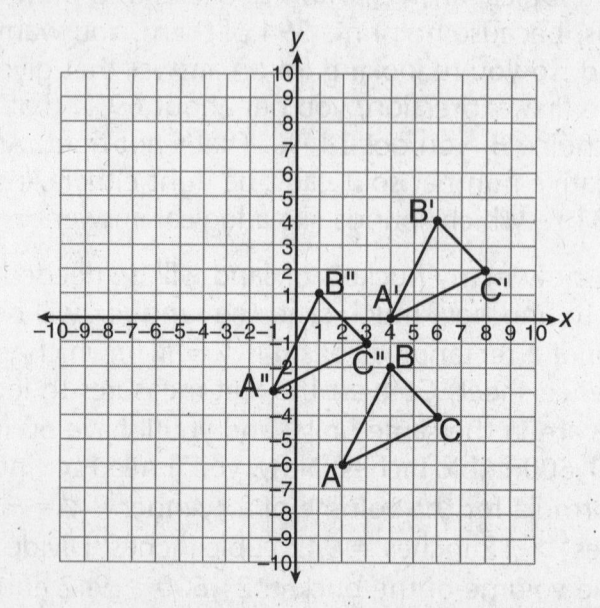

This extended-response question is worth 4 points. A correct 4-point answer to this question would have the triangles graphed as above. The correct vertices of ABC are given as A(2, −6), B(4, −2), and C(6, −4). The correct vertices of A'B'C' are A' (4, 0), B' (6, 4), and C' (8, 2). The correct vertices of A"B"C" are

A" (−1, −3), B" (1, 1), and C" (3, −1). To get full credit for this question, you would not only have to plot all these points correctly but you would also need to state the translation from ABC to A"B"C". For instance, a proper response could be: To translate triangle ABC to A"B"C", you need to move each vertex three units to the left and three units up on the coordinate grid.

20. **C** Putting the expressions into decimal form will make it easier to see the correct order. 0.622 is already in decimal form. $\sqrt{0.49} = 0.7$, $\frac{4}{5} = 0.8$, and $|-0.9| = 0.9$. Now you can see the order of the values. Answer choice **C** lists the expressions in order from least to greatest.

21. **A** Damien moves 200 kilograms of sand on the first day. On the next day, he will move one-quarter of what he moved the first day, or $\frac{1}{4}$ of 200 = 50. On the third day, he will move one-quarter of what he moved on the second day, or $\frac{1}{4}$ of 50 = 12.5. On the fourth day, he will move one-quarter of what he moved on the third day, or $\frac{1}{4}$ of 12.5 or 3.125. Therefore, after four days, Damien will have move 200 + 50 + 12.5 + 3.125 = 265.625, or $265\frac{5}{8}$ kilograms of sand, which is answer choice **A**.

22. **C** To find the correct answer to this question, think of the definition of each type of graph. A bar graph is often used to compare quantities. A box-and-whisker plot is used to summarize data into quartiles, median, and extreme values. A line graph shows change and the direction of the change over a period of time. A scatterplot shows the relationship between two sets of data. To display the temperature change in Beijing, a line graph would be the most appropriate, which is answer choice **C**.

23. **D** Use the reference sheet to find the formula for the area of a rectangle, which is $A = lw$. This will help you to figure out the area of each surface of the box. The front side of the box is 12 inches × 6 inches, or 72 square inches. The back of the box is also 72 square inches. The side of the box is 3 inches × 6 inches = 18 square inches. The other side is also 18 square inches. The top of the box is 12 inches × 3 inches, or 36 square inches. The bottom of the box is also 36 square inches. Add the surface areas together: 72 + 72 + 18 + 18 + 36 + 36 = 252 square inches, which is answer choice **D**.

24. **B** The tree diagram in this question shows all of Hakeem's 16 possible outcomes after both coins are selected. The first step is to assign monetary values to each entry on the tree diagram. For instance, the first outcomes (listed "PP" and "PN") are worth $0.02 and $0.06, respectively. Go down the rest of the list and you will find the values $0.11, $0.26, $0.06, $0.10, $0.15, $0.30, $0.11, $0.15, $0.20, $0.35, $0.26, $0.30, $0.35, and $0.50. Because the question asks for the number of selections equal to $0.35, count the two outcomes that yield such a value: QD and DQ. Two outcomes out of 16 possible outcomes is equivalent to $\frac{2}{16}$, which reduces to $\frac{1}{8}$. That makes **B** the correct answer choice.

25. **D** Triangle PQR has angles of 62° and 28°. The third angle must be equal to 90° because the three angles of a triangle must equal 180°, and 62 + 28 + 90 = 180. For one of the other triangles to be similar to PQR, the interior angles must also be 62°, 28°, and 90°. All of the answer choices are triangles with right angles but only answer choice **D** has an acute angle of 62° and would, therefore, have another acute angle of 28°. Answer choice **D** is correct.

26. **A** The exponent in the scientific notation from this problem is −3. Remove the negative part of the exponent and think of the value of 10^3 first: 10 × 10 × 10 = 1,000. The negative sign means that you make the number into a fraction, or $\frac{1}{1,000}$. If you put this into decimal form, it's equal to 0.001. Now multiply it by 1.8. 0.001 × 1.8 = 0.0018 or answer choice **A**. You can also solve this problem by moving the decimal point 3 places to the left; that would give you the same answer: 0.0018.

27. **B** You may be tempted to choose answer choice **A** because the mean would give an average value, but this might not be the most accurate for the question. The measure of central tendency of the typical birth weight that week would best be represented by the median because a few of the weights were very low. The median would take into consideration the extreme values and indicate the middle value of the set. The mode shows the weight that appears the most often and the range gives the difference between the highest and lowest weight. Answer choice **B** would be the best answer.

28. **A** The inequality $y < 4x - 3$ has a less-than sign, which means that the line of the graph must be dotted. Two of the graphs can be eliminated immediately because they have solid lines and a solid line indicates great-than-or-equal-to or less-than-or-equal-to. Eliminate answer choices **B** and **C** right away. To find out which of the remaining graphs is correct, plug in values from the shaded portion of each graph and see if the inequality works. From answer choice **A**, plug in the coordinates (2, 0): $y < 4x - 3$ or $0 < 4(2) - 3$, or $0 < 5$. That seems to work. Try plugging in coordinates from answer choice **D** to see if they work. Using an easy set of coordinates from the shaded area, (0, 0), you get $y < 4x - 3$, or $0 < 4(0) - 3$ or $0 < -3$. That's not right. That makes **A** the correct answer choice.

29. **B** Simplify the equation to find the right answer.

$$7(9 - 2y) = (y + 8)5$$
$$63 - 14y = 5y + 40$$
$$23 = 19y$$

Answer choice **B** is correct. You could check your answer by solving for the variable, but that would require a good deal of extra work; it might be easier to confirm that your calculations were correct in simplifying the original equation.

30. **B** The formula for the volume of a cylinder is $V = \pi r^2 h$, which you know from the reference sheet. The radius of the cylinder in the figure is 7.8. The square of the radius is 60.84. Now multiply $3.14 \times 60.84 \times 20.4 = 3,897.167$. The question asks for the approximate volume, which would be answer choice **B**, 3,840 cm^3. Another way to find the correct answer choice would be to round the measures. π is approximately 3, the radius is approximately 8, or 64 when squared, and the height is approximately 20. $3 \times 64 \times 20 = 3,840$, which is closest to answer choice **B**.

31. **A** To find the correct answer choice to this question, use Process of Elimination to toss away the untrue statements. Answer choice **A** says that the two triangles are right triangles. You can plug the lengths of triangle ABC into the Pythagorean theorem and see if it works: $6^2 + 8^2 = 10^2$, or $36 + 64 = 100$, or $100 = 100$. Triangle ABC is a right triangle. For triangle XYZ, add the measures of the two angles and see if they equal 90°: $25 + 65 = 90$. They do equal 90°, so the third angle must be 90°. Triangle XYZ is also a right triangle. Answer choice **A** is correct. As always, you should look at the other answer choices to make sure your answer is right.

Answer choice **B** says that the triangles are isosceles. An isosceles triangle has at least two congruent sides. Triangle ABC definitely doesn't have two congruent sides so you can eliminate this answer choice. Answer choice **C** can be eliminated because you've already noted that one triangle doesn't have congruent sides. Answer choice **D** says that the angles of the two triangles are congruent. You are only given enough information to determine that one angle of each triangle is congruent, the 90° angle. Otherwise, there is no way to know if the statement in choice **D** is true or not.

Answers and Explanations for Practice Math OGT 1

32. Katrina had $200 in her bank account and added $300 each week during the summer. An equation to find the amount of money in her account after x weeks would be $K = 200 + 300x$. Evan had $2,650 in his account and spent $50 each week during the summer. An equation to find the amount of money in his account after x weeks would be $E = 2,650 - 50x$. To find the number of weeks until Katrina has more money in her bank account than Evan, use an inequality and solve: $200 + 300x > 2,650 - 50x$. This inequality can be simplified to $350x > 2,450$, or even further to $x > 7$. Katrina will have more in her account after 8 weeks. (Don't forget the inequality does not have a greater-than or equal-to sign.)

Another way to solve this would be to make a table and put in the weekly changes to both accounts.

| Amount in Savings |||
Week	Katrina	Evan
1	500	2,600
2	800	2,550
3	1,100	2,500
4	1,400	2,450
5	1,700	2,400
6	2,000	2,350
7	2,300	2,300
8	2,600	2,250

This question is worth 2 points. You would receive the full 2 points for this question if you had written each equation correctly and you had stated that Katrina would have more money in her bank account after 8 weeks.

33. **A** The way to solve this question is to count the 4-edged faces for each figure. Try visualizing (or even sketching) a model of each figure to help you. A rectangular prism has 6 faces, all of which are 4-edged. A rectangular pyramid has only one 4-edged face, which is its base. A triangular prism has 5 faces but only 3 of them are 4-edged. A triangular pyramid has no 4-edged faces. Answer choice **A**, the rectangular prism, is correct.

34. **D** The side ratio of a 30-60-90 triangle is $s : s\sqrt{3} : 2s$. The side opposite the 30° angle is 20 feet, so the side opposite the 90° angle is 2 × 20 feet, or 40 feet, which is answer choice **D**. If you didn't happen to know the side ratios, you could use the sine function to find the answer. $\sin \angle = \frac{opposite}{hypotenuse}$, which in this case is $\sin 30° = \frac{20}{x}$. That is equal to $0.5 = \frac{20}{x}$, or $x = \frac{20}{0.5}$, which results in a value for x of 40.

35. **B** Place the correct coefficients with each variable, and you should end up with $3.95x + 3.50y$. Set that so that it does not exceed $200, $3.95x + 3.50y \leq 200$, and you will end up with the inequality listed in answer choice **B**. You would need to be careful of the coefficients so that you didn't mix them up and pick answer choice **C**. The picture frames cost $3.95 each and are represented by x. The Frisbees cost $3.50 each and are represented by y. You also needed to find an inequality that indicated that Simone wanted to spend $200 or less. Only answer choice **B** has the coefficients placed correctly and has the inequality sign correct so that Simone can spend up to $200—but not more.

36. **C** If the Good Reading bookstore wants to know how many books are read by people who participate in reading groups that meet in the store, then the survey should include the people in those groups. The only answer choice that says that the survey would involve only people in the reading groups is answer choice **C**. That is the best population to survey to represent the average participant in the reading groups.

37. **A** You know that angle a and the 30° angle are supplementary angles, which means that when added together their measures equal 180°. Therefore, angle a is 180° − 30° = 150°. Opposite interior angles are equivalent, which makes angle b equal to 30°. That makes answer choice **A** correct. You could have eliminated choices **B** and **C** because you can tell that angle a is obtuse by looking at the diagram, and its measure should be much greater than 30°. You could also eliminate answer choice **D** because angles a and b cannot be equal, because one is obtuse and the other is acute.

Answers and Explanations for Practice Math OGT 1

38. **D** The way to find the missing measure is to set up a proportion of the two boxes. Be careful when you set up the proportion. The larger box has a length of 33 centimeters and a width of 24 centimeters, which is a ratio of $\frac{33}{24}$. The smaller box has an unknown length, x, and a width of 8, which is a ratio of $\frac{x}{8}$. Because the boxes have similar proportions, you can set the ratios equal to each other.

$$\frac{33}{24} = \frac{x}{8}$$
$$\frac{264}{24} = x$$
$$11 = x$$

Answer **D** is the correct choice.

39. **D** The best way to answer this question is to look at the graph and determine any kind of visible trend. It appears that whole milk consumption has gone down steadily every five years. Therefore, it is reasonable to expect that in 1965 the figure was higher than it was in 1970. That means it is most likely that the figure is higher than 25, based on how steady the trend is. Answer choice **D**, 29, seems to be the best choice.

40. **B** You are being asked to find the solution to the system of equations $3x = 7y + 1$ and $x = y - 1$. When finding the solution to a system of equations with two variables, you solve one equation for one of the variables and plug the value of that variable into the other equation. In this case, the second equation is already solved for x, so simply plug that value into the first equation and simplify.

$$3(y - 1) = 7y + 1$$
$$3y - 3 = 7y + 1$$
$$-4 = 4y$$
$$-1 = y$$

Now that you know the value of y, you can go back to either of the original equations and substitute -1 in place of y. $x = y - 1$ becomes $x = -1 - 1$, or $x = -2$. The ordered pair that satisfies both equations is $(-2, -1)$, which is answer choice **B**. You can check your answer by substituting the values for x and y into the other equation. You could also have solved this problem is by graphing both equations and finding the point where the lines intersect.

41. This question is asking you which option is the better bargain for Oswald. Compare the two possibilities, as shown below.

    Option 1: 5 shirts costs $100.00.

    Option 2: 15% off the ticketed prices. $25.75 + $21.45 + $18.05 + $24.80 + $29.80 = $119.85. With the 15% discount: $119.85 − 0.15($119.85) = $119.85 − $17.98 = $101.87.

    The better bargain for Oswald would be the 5 shirts for $100.00

    This question is worth 2 points. To earn full credit on this 2-point question, you must correctly identify which deal offers Oswald the better bargain and show your work or provide an explanation.

    If you wanted to provide an explanation, instead of showing your work, you could have said: When the prices of the shirts Oswald wants to buy are reduced by 15%, the sum of the prices is greater than $100.00. Therefore, Oswald will save money by taking the "5-for-$100" deal.

42. **B** You can set up a proportion to solve for the height of the tree in this problem. To do this, you can compare the lengths of the shadow of the tree and the pole to the height of the tree and the pole. The ratio should look like $\frac{420}{120} = \frac{x}{72}$. If you cross multiply, you will get $\frac{30,240}{120} = x$, which reduces to $252 = x$. The tree is 252 inches tall, which is answer choice **B**.

Answers and Explanations for Practice Math OGT 1

43. After you have reflected rectangle DEFG over the x-axis, the rectangle D'E'F'G' will have the coordinates D'(3, −4), E'(7, −4), F'(3, −1), and G'(7,−1).

    Rectangle D"E"F"G" will have the coordinates D"(−3, 4), E"(−7, 4), F"(−3, 1), and G"(−7, 1), as shown below.

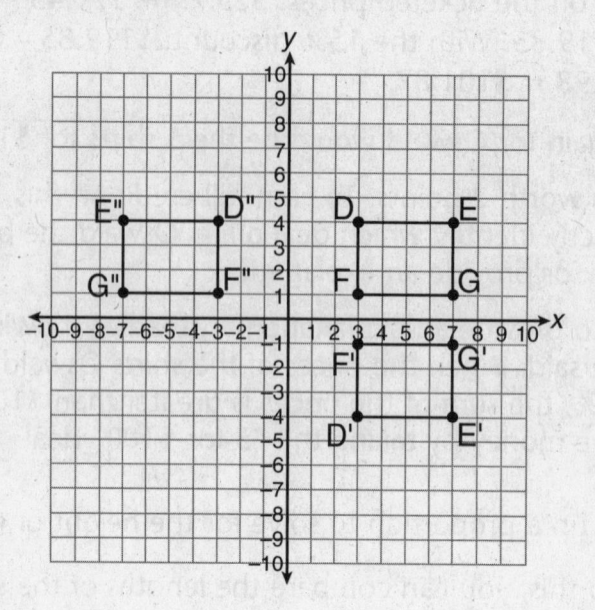

    This is a 4-point question. To receive all 4 points for this question, you would have to correctly graph rectangles DEFG, D'E'F'G', and D"E"F"G" correctly. Then, you would have to describe the mathematical operation used to reflect the coordinates of a figure over the x- and y-axes. An example of the correct description is: To reflect the coordinates of a figure over the x-axis, the y-coordinates of the figure must be multiplied by −1. To reflect the coordinates of a figure over the y-axis, the x-coordinate must be multiplied by −1.

44. **A** This question is asking you to match an equation with a corresponding graph that has already been created. The equation in this question is $y = 1 + x^2$. x^2 can never be negative because $-1^2 = 1$, $-2^2 = 4$, and so on. So regardless of what the x-coordinate is in this graph, the y-coordinate is always positive. Already you know that the correct answer choice must be **A**, because it's the only graph that doesn't show any points with negative values for the y-coordinate. Plug in some values to see if you're right. When $x = -1$, $y = 2$. When $x = 0$, $y = 2$. When $x = -1$, $y = 2$. That's about right for the graph in answer choice **A**.

Answers and Explanations for Practice Math OGT 2

ANSWERS AND EXPLANATIONS FOR PRACTICE MATH OGT 2

1. **B** You need to find the dimensions of Leti's bedroom. The perimeter of her bedroom is given as 38 feet. She has four strings of lights, two are 8 feet long and two are 12 feet long. Don't be fooled into choosing answer choice **C** automatically because that only lists the lengths of the lights. First, find the perimeter of a room that has those dimensions. $P = 2l + 2w$, or $2(8) + 2(12)$, or 40 feet. That can't be the right answer because the perimeter of the room is only 38 feet. Use POE to find the right answer. You can eliminate answer choice **A** because one dimension is 14 feet so it is too long for the 12 foot string of lights. Answer choice **B** could work so find the perimeter. $P = 2(7) + 2(12) = 14 + 24 = 38$ feet. That looks like the correct choice. Check answer choice **D** to be sure. The dimensions make the perimeter equal to 38 feet, but the 8-foot string of lights won't fit on the 9-foot wall. You can eliminate this choice too. Answer choice **B** is correct.

2. **A** You want to determine the inequality that will give the senior class a profit of at least $470. They will charge $2.50 per ride, which is $2.5r$. The Ferris wheel will cost $260 to rent so you would deduct that from the money they would make for the rides: $2.5r - 260$. Now you have to figure out which inequality sign to use. Because the class wants to make $470 or more, you would use the greater than or equal to sign, $\geq$. The correct answer is answer choice **A**: $2.5r - 260 \geq 470$.

3. **C** To find the answer to this problem, you need to find the total of all the food that is bought, and then add 7% sales tax. Three orders of fries is $3 \times 2.60 = \$7.80$. Two orders of onion rings is $2 \times 3.10 = \$6.20$. Six tuna melts is $6 \times 6.50 = \$39.00$. And $6 \times 1.50 = \$9.00$. Add them together: $7.80 + 6.20 + 39.00 + 9.00 = \$62.00$. Multiply the total by 7%. $62 \times 0.07 = \$4.34$. Now add the tax. $\$62.00 + \$4.34 = \$66.34$. Answer choice **C** is correct.

4. **C** The rocket-powered race car took one minute and 45 seconds and 1,050 feet to stop, once the parachute had ejected. First, you will need to calculate the total number of seconds: one minute and 45 seconds is equal to $60 + 45$, or 105 seconds. To find the rate of feet per second divide: 1050 feet $\div$ 105 seconds = 10. The car stopped at a rate of 10 feet per second, which is answer choice **C**.

5. **B** One way to find the answer to this question is to substitute numbers into the equation to see what happens. Say the distance is 100 feet. Divided that by 20 seconds. $V = \frac{100}{20} = 5$ feet per second. Now decrease the time to 10 seconds: $V = \frac{100}{10} = 10$ feet per second. So, as the time decreases, the velocity increases. That means answer choice **B** is correct.

6. **C** The range of a box-and-whisker plot is the difference between the extreme values. The least value is the end of the left whisker, which is 33. The greatest value is the end of the right whisker, which is 100. Now find the difference: 100 − 33 = 67, which is answer choice **C**.

7. To solve this problem fully, you need to find the slopes of $\overline{AD}$ and $\overline{BC}$, as well as determine if the points on the graph form a trapezoid. Remember that a trapezoid is a quadrilateral that has two parallel sides. If two of the sides are parallel, they will have the same slope. You can tell by looking at the graph that $\overline{AB}$ and $\overline{CD}$ are not parallel so you do not need to find their slopes. You want to find the slope of $\overline{AD}$ and $\overline{BC}$. Use the slope formula: $m = \frac{y_2 - y_1}{x_2 - x_1}$. $\overline{BC} = \frac{4-2}{2-(-2)} = \frac{2}{4} = \frac{1}{2}$. The slope of line $\overline{BC}$ is $\frac{1}{2}$. Now find the slope of $\overline{AD}$: $\frac{2-(-2)}{5-(-3)} = \frac{4}{8} = \frac{1}{2}$. The slope of line $\overline{AD}$ is also $\frac{1}{2}$. Because the slopes are the same, the lines are parallel. That means figure ABCD is a trapezoid.

This question is worth 4 points. To receive full credit for this question your answer needed to show the slopes for both $\overline{AD}$ and $\overline{BC}$, with proper work that shows how you found them, and a correct answer and explanation as to why the shape is a trapezoid. An acceptable response could be, "Yes, the figure is a trapezoid because it is a quadrilateral and the slope of lines $\overline{AD}$ and $\overline{BC}$ are the same so the lines are parallel."

8. **B** To find the answer to this question, it helps to put each of the numbers in the table into the same form. The number of convertibles would go from $\frac{120,000}{100}$ to 1,200. The one-hundred thousand minivans would become 100,000. The 1.2 million compact cars would become 1,200,000. And the number of SUVs would go from 1.02×10^5 to 102,000. In order from least to greatest, they would be the convertible (1,200), minivans (100,000), SUVs (102,000), and compact cars (1,200,000). This is answer choice **B**.

9. **C** Hansel received a mean or average score of 93% on two tests, which means he could have scored a 93 and a 93, a 94 and a 92, or any other two scores that add up to $96 \times 2 = 112$. It's important to remember that there are two tests giving a 93% mean. Now, the next three test scores are $85\% + 94\% + 70\% = 249$. Here's where you add in the two test scores above: $249 + 112 = 435$. Divide this by five tests to get the mean: $435 \div 5 = 87$. The mean score of all five tests is 87, or answer choice **C**.

10. **A** You are given the coordinates of the center of a circle and a point that the circle passes through. If you connect these two points, you will have a radius of the circle. To find the radius, you would use the distance formula, which is $d = \sqrt{(x_2 - x_1)^2 + (y_2 - y_1)^2}$ and plug in the coordinates. $d = \sqrt{(3-(-2))^2 + (4-(-1))^2}$ or $\sqrt{(3+2)^2 + (4+1)^2}$, which is answer choice **A**.

11. **B** To find which of the points on the number line that best represents $\sqrt{20}$, you should find the square root and round to the nearest tenth. The square root of 20 is 4.4721..., which rounds up to 4.5. The point on the number line that is nearest to 4.5 is point B. The correct answer choice is **B**.

12. **D** This question requires you to find the height of the skyscraper. You are given an angle and the adjacent length, and you need to find the opposite length. Remember the trigonometric abbreviation of SOHCAHTOA to help you find the function you should use. You would use tangent: $\tan \angle = \frac{opposite}{adjacent}$, or $\tan 84.5 = \frac{x}{100}$. That is equal to $10.39 \times 100 = x$, or 1,039 feet $= x$. The correct answer choice is **D**.

Answers and Explanations for Practice Math OGT 2

13. **C** Heather bought a sweater that was $38 and on sale for 15% off. The new price of the sweater is equal to $38 − ($38 × 0.15) = $38.00 − $5.70, or $32.30. Now you can add the 8% sales tax: $32.30 + ($32.30 × 0.08) = $32.30 + $2.58 = $34.88. This makes answer choice **C** correct.

14. **B** The Venn diagram shows that some isosceles triangles are also acute triangles. You have to find the triangle in the answer choices that shows a triangle that is both an isosceles triangle and an acute triangle. Use POE to find the right answer. The triangle in answer choice **A** is isosceles because two of its angles are equal, but it is not an acute triangle because one angle is greater than 90°. Eliminate that answer choice. Answer choice **B** shows a triangle with two equal angles, so it is isosceles. It also has three acute angles. This looks like the correct answer choice. Check the other choices to be sure. Answer choice **C** shows two equal angles but the third angle is 90°. An acute triangle has three angles that are each less than 90°. This isn't the correct choice. Eliminate it. Answer choice **D** doesn't have two equal angles or three acute angles. Eliminate this choice. You're left with answer choice **B**.

15. **B** Remember the definition of similar triangles: They have identical shapes, their corresponding angles are equal, and their corresponding sides are proportional. Because their corresponding angles must be equal, you know that the measure of $\angle a = \angle A$. Both are 32°, which is answer choice **B**.

16. **D** To solve this problem, you first have to determine the probability for each color so that you have a basis for Jacob's spins. When Alexis spins, the arrow lands on white 5 out of 20 spins. That ratio is $\frac{5}{20}$, which is $\frac{1}{4}$ or about 25% of the time. When Matthew spins, the arrow lands on white 5 out of 30 spins. That ratio is $\frac{5}{30}$, which is $\frac{1}{6}$ or about 16% of the time. When Rachael spins, the arrow lands on the white 8 out of 40 spins. That ratio is $\frac{8}{40}$, which is $\frac{1}{5}$ or about 20% of the time. Use an average of the three percents for when Jacob spins, roughly 20%.

When Jacob spins, the arrow should land on white about 20% of the time. 20% of 60 is 12. You've narrowed the answer choices down to **C** or **D**. Now go to the purple section and see how many times the arrow lands on it for each spinner. Alexis is 9 out of 20, or 45%; Matthew is 16 out of 30 or 53%; and Rachael is 20 out of 40, or 50%. When Jacob spins, the arrow should land on purple about 50% of 60 spins, or about 30 times. Answer choice **D** has 29 for purple. That looks like the right answer choice. You should try the other colors, just to be sure. For black, Alexis has 3 out of 20, or 15%; Matthew has 3 out of 30, or 10%; and Rachael has 5 out of 40, or 12.5%. That means

Jacob will have about 13% of 60 spins, or about 8. Answer choice **D** is still looking good. Try the green: Alexis spun 3 out of 20, or about 15%; Matthew landed on green 6 out of 30, or about 20%; and Rachael landed on green 7 out of 40, or about 17.5%. Jacob's arrow should land on green about 18% of the time, or about 11 times. Answer choice **D** is 12 for green. Answer choice **D** is correct.

17. **B** The expression $(x^4) \times (3x^2) \times (2x^2)$ can be factored to find the simplest form: $x \cdot x \cdot x \cdot x \cdot 3 \cdot x \cdot x \cdot 2 \cdot x \cdot x = 3 \cdot 2 \cdot x^8 = 6x^8$. You can also find the answer by adding the exponents of the powers that have the same base. The base in this expression is x, so add the powers $4 + 2 + 2 = 8$. But don't forget to multiply the coefficients $3 \times 2 = 6$. Answer choice **B** is correct.

18. An appropriate graph for displaying the winning times in the Women's 100-meter dash would be a line graph. You need to create a graph, as shown below.

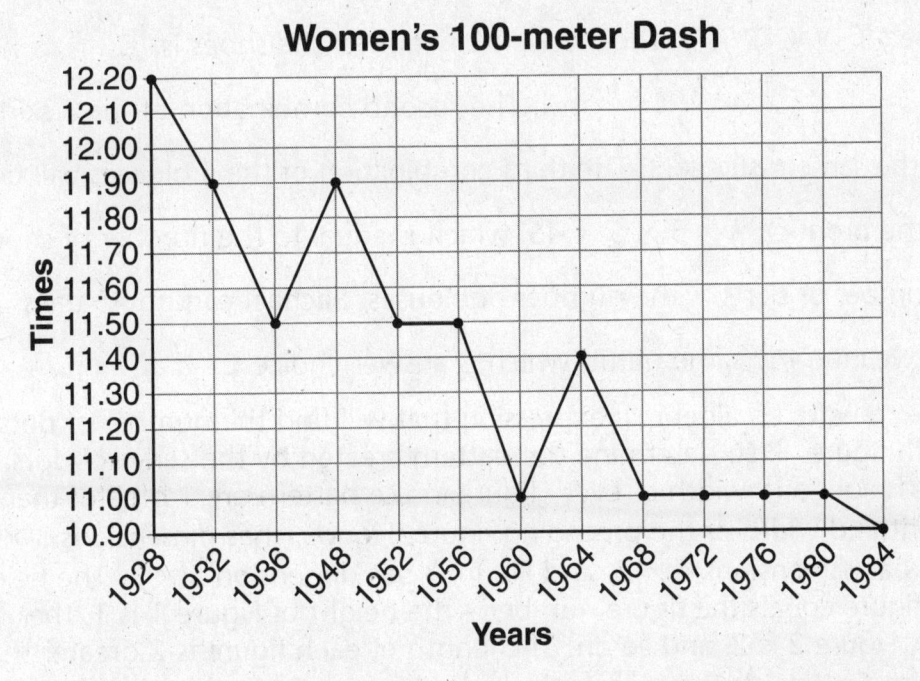

Women's 100-meter Dash

You also need to explain why you used this particular graph. You could say that you used a line graph because it was the best way to display the changes in the winning times in the Olympic Women's 100-meter race over time.

This question is worth 4 points. To get full credit, you need to create a proper and accurate graph based on the data in the problem, as well as provide an appropriate explanation as to why you used that particular graph.

Answers and Explanations for Practice Math OGT 2

19. **D** You need to find the length of the railing that will go around the porch and terrace of the Walker's house. The radius of the circular terrace is 5 feet. The railing would go around the terrace so you would need to find the circumference of the circle. (Check the reference sheet for the formula!)

    $C = 2\pi r$, or $2 \times \pi \times 5$ feet = 31.4 feet. Part of the circle is within the rectangular porch area so subtract that portion, which is one-quarter of the circle: $31.4 \div 4 = 7.85$. Taking away that portion, you get $31.4 - 7.85 = 23.55$ feet of railing. The rectangular area is 10 feet along one side, 17 feet along the back (22 feet – 5 feet), and 10 feet plus the 5 feet for the other side. $10 + 17 + 15 = 42$ feet. The total amount of railing needed is 23.55 feet + 42 feet = 65.55 feet, or about 66 feet. Answer choice **D** is correct.

20. **C** The order of when Rachael would wear the outfits isn't important, so you need to find the answer with the product of combinations. The combinations would be $(^3C^1)(^3C^1)(^5C^1)$. The first combination of the shoes is $^3C^1 = \frac{3!}{(3-1)!1!} = \frac{3 \cdot 2 \cdot 1}{2!} = \frac{3 \cdot 2 \cdot 1}{2 \cdot 1} = 3$. The second combination of the 3 skirts will get the same result of 3. The third combination of the 5 blouses will be 5. Find the product: $3 \times 3 \times 5 = 45$, which is equal to the number of shoes × the number of skirts × the number of blouses. Rachael can go 45 days without wearing the same outfit, which is answer choice **C**.

21. You have to write an algebraic expression that will find the number of dots in the *n*th figure. First, determine the pattern created by the series of dots. Both the height and width of every figure in the pattern are 1 greater than the height and width of the preceding figure. Figure 1 has dimensions 3×1, Figure 2 has dimensions 4×2, and Figure 3 has dimension 5×3. The height of each figure equals the figure number – the height of Figure 1 is 1, the height of Figure 2 is 2, and so on. The length of each figure is 2 greater than the height. So, the algebraic formula would be $(n + 2) \times n$.

    The 20th figure would be 20 higher than its number $(n + 2)$ or $(20 + 2) = 22$. The figure's length would be the same as its number, or 20. $22 \times 20 = 440$ dots.

    This question is worth 2 points. To get full credit for this question, you would need to write the formula and plug in the values for the 20th figure: $(n + 2) \times n = (20 + 2) \times 20 = 22 \times 20 = 440$ dots.

22. **A** To solve this question, you can set up a proportion and find one part of your answer immediately. One meter is equal to one million micrometers, and you want to know the value of 17 micrometers in meters. Set up the proportion of meters on one side and micrometers on the other: $\frac{x}{1} = \frac{17}{1,000,000}$, or $x = \frac{17}{1,000,000}$. Just knowing that much, you can eliminate two of the answer choices, **C** and **D**. Now, put the fraction into decimal form. $\frac{17}{1,000,000} = 0.000017$. That looks like the first part of answer choice **A**. Put 181 micrometers into decimal form: $\frac{181}{1,000,000} = 0.000181$. Now it looks like answer choice **A** is correct. You can put each of the decimals into scientific notation, just to be sure: $0.000017 = 1.7 \times 10^{-5}$ and $0.000181 = 1.81 \times 10^{-4}$. Answer choice **A** is correct.

23. **C** For this question, you need to find the number of students who scored an 80 or above. So you should look at the test scores for 81–90 (there are 6 students in this range) and the test scores for 91–100 (there are 5 students in this range). Add the numbers together: $6 + 5 = 11$. Answer choice **C** is correct.

24. **C** To find the number of times Juan can take the bus and still leave himself $1,475 for a deposit on a car, plug the values into the equation: $1,475 = -2.5x + 1,625$. Now, solve the equation. $-150 = -2.5x$ or $60 = x$. Juan can take 60 rides on the bus and still have enough for the deposit on a car, which is answer choice **C**.

25. **D** You can find the table that is correct by plugging the values into the equation, $y = x^2 + 1$. The first set of coordinates in answer choice **A** is $(-3, 9)$: $9 = 9(-3)^2 + 1$, or $9 = 9 + 1$, or $9 = 10$. That's not right, so eliminate answer choice **A**. Answer choice **B** has the first coordinates of $(-3, -8)$. You already learned that a value of -3 for x would result in a value of 10 for y. This means only **D** has the right set of numbers for the first set of coordinates. If you look at the coordinates in answer choice **D**, you can see how the graph will form a parabola, with the y-coordinates going from 10 to 1 and back to 10. Answer choice **D** is correct.

26. You are given a table with the number of hours that three students spent watching television over a 4-week period. You are to find the mean for each student and then the mean for the entire set of data.

    The mean for Tricia: 15 + 18 + 13 + 20 = 66 ÷ 4 = 16.5.
    The mean for Jose: 9 + 12 + 11 + 14 = 46 ÷ 4 = 11.5.
    The mean for Rosa: 11 + 13 + 8 + 12 = 44 ÷ 4 = 11.

    Find the mean for the entire set of data: 15 + 18 + 13 + 20 + 9 + 12 + 11 + 14 + 11 + 13 + 8 + 12 = 156 ÷ 12 = 13. 13 is the mean for the entire set of data.

    This question is worth 2 points. To get full credit for this question you would need to show how you found the mean for each student (as above) and clearly label the mean for each. Then you would need to show how you found the mean for the entire set of data and label the answer.

27. **D** You can use POE to find the right answer to this question. The first answer choice is $d = t - 2$. Plug in the values from the table. $3 = 1 - 2$, or $3 = -1$. This did not work, so eliminate answer choice **A**. The next equation is $d = t + 2$. Use the same values: $3 = 1 + 2$, or $3 = 3$. Go to the next set in the table: $6 = 2 + 2$, or $6 = 4$. Eliminate answer choice **B**. The next equation is $d = t^2 - 2$. Go back to the first set of values: $3 = 1^2 - 2$, or $3 = -1$. This doesn't work either, so eliminate answer choice **C**. Answer choice **D** must be correct but check all of the values, just to be sure: $d = t^2 + 2$ or $3 = 1^2 + 2$, or $3 = 3$. Plug in the next set to double-check: $6 = 2^2 + 2$ or $6 = 6$. It looks like it works!

28. **C** You have to use the graph to determine which answer choice is true. Get rid of the choices which can't be supported. Answer choice **A** says that financial responsibility has always been evenly divided. But even through 1998, more homes were put in the man's name, so you can't prove that financial responsibility was evenly divided. Answer choice **B** says that the male population has decreased. That type of information can't be found in the graph. Answer choice **C** says that women are gradually taking more financial responsibility. The number of women who have homes put in their names has increased over time, and that does show a gradual additional financial responsibility. This looks like the right answer. Check the last to be sure. Answer choice **D** says that by the year 2007, the male and female graphs will be the same. This doesn't look likely, because based on the graph, the male and female graphs will take much longer than that to be equal. Answer choice **C** is correct.

Roadmap to the Ohio Graduation Test: Mathematics

29. **D** You are to find the expression that equals $(-p) \times (r)$. All of the choices use absolute value and one way to find the correct answer is to plug in actual numbers for the variables. Use 2 for p and 3 for r. $(-p) \times (r) = (-2) \times 3 = -6$. Now do the same for the other expression in each answer choice. $|(-p) \times r| = |(-2) \times 3| = |-6| = 6$. That's not right. Eliminate that choice. Answer choice **B** is $|-pr| = |-(2)(3)| = |-6| = 6$. That's not right either. Check the next answer choice: $|-p(-r)| = |-2(-3)| = |6| = 6$. Eliminate that one. The correct answer must be answer choice **D** but check it to be sure. $-|(-p) \times r| = -|(-2) \times 3| = -|-6| = -6$. That matches the original expression so it's right.

30. **C** To find the value of x, use the area formula (which can be found in your reference sheet), $A = lw$. $4 = (x-5)(x-2)$. Now solve for x. $4 = x - 5$, or $9 = x$. Solve the other part: $4 = x - 2$ or $6 = x$. Now plug those values back into the original formula and see which one works. $4 = (9-5)(9-2)$, or $4 = 4 \times 7$ or $4 = 28$. That doesn't work. Try the other value: $4 = (6-5)(6-2)$, or $4 = 1 \times 4$ which is equal to $4 = 4$. The correct value of x is 6, which is answer choice **C**.

31. **A** The way to find what percent of Damien's pennies is left is to put all of the values into the same form. Because the answer choices are in the percent form, use that form. 55% is already in the percent form. $0.25 = 25\%$ and $\frac{1}{10} = 10\%$. Now, add them all together: $55\% + 25\% + 10\% = 90\%$. That means that there is 10% left, because $100\% - 90\% = 10\%$. Answer choice **A** is correct.

32. **C** Use substitution to find the answer to this question. The mass remains the same. Use 10 for the mass then plug different numbers into the volume to see how the density changes. First, use a volume of 20: $D = \frac{10}{20}$ or $\frac{1}{2}$. Increase the volume to 100: $D = \frac{10}{100}$, or $\frac{1}{10}$. So, as the volume increases, the density decreases. The graph that shows that relationship is answer choice **C**.

Answers and Explanations for Practice Math OGT 2

33. **B** You are given four polyhedra and asked to find the one where the formula $V = lwh$ would apply to find its volume. This formula is based on a rectangular base which has length and width. All of the figures in the answer choices cannot use the area of a rectangle formula, except answer choice **B**. For example, the tetrahedron in answer choice **C** has a triangular base and would use the formula $V = \frac{1}{3}Bh$ to find the volume, where **B** is the area of the base. The correct answer is answer choice **B**.

34. One juice company has the same gross income, even though its customer base is half the size. You have to explain how this could be. Well, you are told that each person spent $2.88 per juice for the first juice company. If the customers spent twice as much per juice for the second company, $5.76, then they would be able to earn the same amount.

    This question is worth 2 points. To receive full credit for this question, you would have to state that the second juice company needed to charge more for its juice, and explain your reasoning with numbers to prove how they could have the same gross income.

35. **D** You are being asked to find the dimensions of a pencil case that would hold 30 pencils that are 10 centimeters in length. You already know one of the dimensions: the case would need to be 10 centimeters long. You can eliminate answer choices **A** and **B**. Multiply the width of each pencil by the number of pencils: $0.9 \times 30 = 27$ centimeters. You need a box that has a width and height to fit 27 centimeters. Answer choice **C** has a width and height of 6×4, or 24 centimeters. That's too small. Answer choice **D** has a width and height of 9×3, or 27 centimeters. That's exactly what you're looking for. The correct answer is answer choice **D**.

36. **D** You are looking for the volume of each of the containers to see how many tubes would contain the same amount of shredded paper as the box. The box is 4 feet by 2.5 feet by 2 feet. Plug those values into the formula $V = lwh$: $V = 4 \text{ feet} \times 2.5 \text{ feet} \times 2 \text{ feet} = 20$ cubic feet. The tube is 1.5 feet long and has a diameter of 1 foot. Use $V = \pi r^2 h$: $V = 3.14 \times (0.5 \text{ ft})^2 \times 1.5 \text{ ft} = 1.1775 \text{ ft}^3$. Now divide the volume of the box by the volume of the tube: $\frac{20}{1.1775} = 16.985$, or about 17, which is answer choice **D**.

37. **B** This question is asking you to find the percentage of seniors who attended the pep rally. To find the answer you would add the numbers of all who attended the rally and then divide the number of seniors by the total. 350 + 550 + 450 + 400 = 1,750. 400 ÷ 1,750 = 0.228, or approximately 23%. The correct answer is answer choice **B**.

38. **A** Remember SOHCAHTOA to find the answer to this question. The diagram shows you the opposite and adjacent lengths of the angle. To find the measure of ∠A, you would use the tangent formula: $\tan A = \frac{opposite}{adjacent}$, or $\tan A = \frac{25}{40}$. Answer choice **A** is correct.

39. The Tri-Village Baseball League gave away baseballs and bumper stickers to some of the 5,726 fans who attended their game. Every 25th paying customer got a team-signed baseball so 5,726 ÷ 25 = 229.08. They gave away 229 baseballs. Every 10th paying customer received a bumper sticker, so 5,726 ÷ 10 = 572.6. The team gave away 572 bumper stickers. (Be careful not to round up because they didn't give away a bumper sticker until they got to the tenth person.)

    The next part of the question wants you to determine which the greater expense to the team: the baseballs or the bumper stickers. The 229 baseballs they gave away cost $3.99 each: 229 × 3.99 = $913.71. The 572 bumper stickers they gave away cost $1.50 each: 572 × 1.50 = $858. The baseballs cost the team more to give away.

    This question is worth 2 points. To receive full credit for this question, you would have to show how many baseballs and how many bumper stickers were given away, with the numbers clearly labeled. For the second part, you could have shown your work to indicate which give away cost the team more, with everything clearly labeled, or you could have given an explanation such as, "The baseballs cost the team $913.71 to give away, which is more than the $858 that the bumper stickers cost them."

40. **C** Quadrilateral EVOL is reflected over the y-axis, and you are to determine its new vertices. When points are reflected over the y-axis, the x-coordinate is multiplied by −1 and the y-coordinate remains the same. Take each of the vertices and multiply the x-coordinate by −1: (0, 7) remains (0, 7), because 0 × −1 = 0; (2, 8) becomes (−2, 8); (4, 6) becomes (−4, 8); and (0, 1) remains (0, 1). These new vertices are contained in answer choice **C**.

Answers and Explanations for Practice Math OGT 2

41. **B** You have to find the lines that are parallel and perpendicular to the graph of line $y = -\frac{5}{8}x + 6$. Because the given line is already in the slope-intercept form, you know that a line parallel to it will have the same slope of $-\frac{5}{8}$. Eliminate answer choices **C** and **D**. Two lines are perpendicular if the product of their slopes is –1 so the slope of the new line would have to be $\frac{8}{5}$, because $-\frac{5}{8} \times \frac{8}{5} = -1$. The perpendicular line would have a slope of $\frac{8}{5}$. The second equation in answer choice **A** is not the opposite reciprocal and is incorrect.

    Both of the equations in answer choice **B** are correct.

42. **C** Three streets in Dayton are cut by West Fairview Avenue. You have to determine which of the resulting angles are congruent. When parallel lines are intersected by a transversal, the congruent angles are the alternate interior, the alternate exterior, and the corresponding angles. Answer choice **A** says that angles 1 and 3 are congruent. You can eliminate this choice because the angles are neither alternate nor corresponding. Answer choice **B** says that angles 2 and 5 are congruent. Eliminate this choice because they are not corresponding and one is an exterior and the other an interior angle. Answer choice **C** says that angles 3 and 6 are congruent. Those are alternate interior angles so this looks like the correct answer. Check answer choice **D** to be sure. Angles 4 and 8 are not corresponding and one is an interior angle and the other an exterior angle. The correct answer choice is **C**.

43. Bonnie worked at a restaurant and was taxed on her regular pay but not on her tips. She was also paid time and a half for any hours she worked over 30 hours. Time and a half is $1\frac{1}{2}$ times her hourly wage, or $6 \times 1\frac{1}{2} = \$9$. To find what she took home, first find the number of hours she worked. $7\frac{1}{2} + 5\frac{3}{4} + 6 + 5\frac{1}{4} + 9\frac{1}{2} = 34$ hours. Multiply the 30 hours by her regular pay, $30 \times \$6 = \$180$, and then multiply the remaining 4 hours by the time and a half rate, $4 \times \$9 = \$36$. So her wages are $\$180 + \$36 = \$216$.

    She is taxed 12% of her gross pay, which is equal to $\$216 \times 0.12 = \$25.92$.

    The total amount of pay that Bonnie made from the hourly wage is $\$216 - \$25.92 = \$190.08$.

Now find how much Bonnie made in tips: 53.50 + 25.75 + 33 + 34.50 + 68.75 = $215.50. Add that to her wages after taxes: 215.50 + 190.08 = $405.58.

This question is worth 2 points. To receive full credit for this question, you would need to show all of your work or to give an explanation such as, "Bonnie took home $405.58 because she made $215.50 in tips and her wages after taxes were $190.08."

44. **D** For this question you have to find the measure of the central angle between the hour hand and the minute hand. The clock is divided into 12 sections, demarcated by each hour. You can find the measure of each hour by dividing the degrees in a circle by 12: 360 ÷ 12 = 30. So, if the minute hand was on one, the angle would be 30°. In the diagram, the minute hand is on the 4, adding multiply 30° × 4, which is 120. The central angle is about 120°, or answer choice **D**.

The Princeton Review

Partnering with You to Measurably Improve Student Achievement

Our proven 3-step approach lets you **assess** student performance, **analyze** the results, and **act** to improve every student's mastery of skills covered by the Ohio Standards of Learning.

Assess
Deliver formative and benchmark tests

Analyze
Review in-depth performance reports and implement ongoing professional development

Act
Utilize after school programs, course materials, and enrichment resources

Order Roadmap books for your classroom or school.

Call 1-800-REVIEW-2 • E-mail K12sales@review.com • Visit educators.princetonreview.com

If students need to know it, it's in our Roadmap Guides!

Roadmap to the Ohio Graduation Test: Mathematics
0-375-76578-2 • $16.00

Roadmap to the Ohio Graduation Test: Reading
0-375-76579-0 • $16.00

Roadmap to 4th Grade Math, Ohio Edition
0-375-75593-4 • $14.95

Roadmap to 4th Grade Reading and Writing, Ohio Edition
0-375-75594-2 • $14.95

Roadmap to 4th Grade Science, Ohio Edition
0-375-76242-6 • $14.95

Roadmap to 4th Grade Social Studies, Ohio Edition
0-375-75595-0 • $14.95

Roadmap to 6th Grade Math, Ohio Edition
0-375-75597-7 • $14.95

Roadmap to 6th Grade Reading and Writing, Ohio Edition
0-375-75596-9 • $14.95

Roadmap to 6th Grade Science, Ohio Edition
0-375-75599-3 • $14.95

Roadmap to 6th Grade Social Studies, Ohio Edition
0-375-75598-5 • $14.95

The Princeton Review

Available at your local bookstore